Awake, Awake

Awake, Awake

Subversive Feminine Voices in the Jewish Tradition

Dvora Lederman-Daniely

WIPF & STOCK · Eugene, Oregon

AWAKE, AWAKE
Subversive Feminine Voices in the Jewish Tradition

Copyright © 2022 Dvora Lederman-Daniely. All rights reserved. Except for brief quotations in critical publications or reviews, no part of this book may be reproduced in any manner without prior written permission from the publisher. Write: Permissions, Wipf and Stock Publishers, 199 W. 8th Ave., Suite 3, Eugene, OR 97401.

Wipf & Stock
An Imprint of Wipf and Stock Publishers
199 W. 8th Ave., Suite 3
Eugene, OR 97401

www.wipfandstock.com

PAPERBACK ISBN: 978-1-6667-4887-1
HARDCOVER ISBN: 978-1-6667-4888-8
EBOOK ISBN: 978-1-6667-4889-5

08/26/22

This is a book of women's stories, held out as markers along the path. They are for you to read and contemplate in order to assist you toward your own natural-won freedom.
—CLARISSA PINKOLA ESTES, *Women Run with Wolves*

Contents

Preface | 1

Chapter 1: Sexual Politics in the Biblical Narrative | 7
Chapter 2: From an Angel to a Lethal Monster: Transformation and Subversion in the Story of Biblical Yael | 12
Chapter 3: Hanna the Maccabee: A Healing and Restorative Memory of Biblical Esther's Sexual Abuse | 30
Chapter 4: "If Anything but Death Parts Me from You"—The Love of Ruth and Naomi | 43
Chapter 5: Miriam the Prophetess: Bold Oppositional Leader | 59
Chapter 6: Pharoah's Daughter and Zipporah: The Courage to Violate the Patriarchal Decree | 76
Chapter 7: Sarah: The Fight for the Matriarchal Legacy | 86
Chapter 8: The Lover in Song of Songs: Sexual Boldness and Subversive Feminine Pleasure | 98
Chapter 9: Epilogue | 112

Bibliography | 115

Preface

"As a committed Jew, I come to ancient canonical stories with an assumption that I belong to them and they belong to me. I encounter them searching for Torah, that is, for redemptive teaching, and for zikaron, for the collective memory. What happens, however, when I reach out to stories whose worlds do not permit me to enter, that exclude me or distort me? How do we face a story that defaces some of us and thereby diminishes all of us?"[1]

THESE WORDS BY RACHEL Adler, a central thinker in feminist Jewish theology, reflect the viewpoint of several feminist researchers,[2] who contend that female characters in the Bible are mostly marginal in relation to the males—voiceless, erased, obedient, submissive and silenced. On rare occasions, when they do appear as protagonists or central characters, they are typically presented as supporting the hegemonic order and patriarchal rule, rather than challenging them.

So, the question arising is whether the women in the religion of Israel were indeed marginal, mostly supplementing, adjunct to

---

1. Adler, Engendered Judaism, 33.
2. Trible, "Depatriarchalizing in Biblical Interpretation," 217–40; Fuchs, "Who Is Hiding the True?," 137–44; Bird, "The Place of Women in the Israelite Culture," 397–419; Exum, "Second Thoughts about Secondary Characters," 75–88.

the male on his heroic quest? The assumption of this study is that the biased representation of women in the Bible stems from various reasons, which do not necessarily correspond to the religious or political reality prevailing at that time.[3] It is presumed that feminine traditions, in which women were principal and dominant, bolder and more active, have existed and were passed on by word of mouth from one generation to another. Yet, in the later stages of editing the Bible and recording the ancient traditions—tasks that were ostensibly done only by men—the stories have changed, and the female voices were diminished. The authors and editors, by nature of their gender, wrote and edited from a perspective and an outlook that reflects the male experience and reality.[4]

Therefore, the experience of revelation and encounter with the divine voice is also narrated and documented from the male world of images, language and functions. In addition, it is assumed that the traditions were edited in accordance with the needs of the patriarchal order and the dominant ideologies. Thus, the stories of the brave, bold, chosen, leading, central female saviors were diminished, silenced, or partly erased.

Therefore, to fully uncover the female voice, through the mechanisms of reduction, oppression and diminution, the canonical texts must be read as gendered texts. Such a reading will consider the influence of the author/narrator's gender, religion, and social class on his decisions on issues, such as what should be told, and what should be silenced and denied.

The second step in this revisionist process is the identification and neutralization of the mechanisms of reduction and silencing, while attempting to reconstruct and rediscover the erased and silenced voice. This stage, as described in this book, is based on literary theories dealing with the way the voice of the minority group preserves itself within the hegemonic voice. The female voice, according to these theories, is fully uncovered only when we unearth the double, covert and hidden layer that characterizes

---

3. See Meyers, "Women and the Domestic Economy of Early Israel," 36.

4. Ross and Gellman, "Implications of Feminism on Orthodox Jewish Theology," 441–43.

Preface

the feminine voice within the patriarchal texts.[5] The researcher Elaine Showalter[6] argued that women live their lives as doubles: they are members of the general culture, but also take part in a "women's culture"—a sphere of unique experiences and emotions. In a patriarchal culture, the female experience is supervised by the ruling group, and any experience that is not consistent with male models is considered as a deviation, as inessential, and is therefore ignored and silenced. Therefore, women, as a silent group, must regulate their forms of experiences and language through the forms that are permitted in the ruling structure. Beyond this regularization, women have no choice but to channel the language of their authentic culture out of the authorized frameworks into the "wilderness." The "wilderness" is an abandoned, unclassified, unregulated, undefined sphere in the hegemonic and symbolic order, and is perceived as an undeciphered black hole. In other words, the female voice, and hence the female text, is a double voice, and should be read as two alternative texts. One text is the overt, disciplined and compliant text, but underneath it, under the veil of encryption and covering, lies another text that speaks from the undisciplined wilderness. Giving heed this text, which speaks from the experiential spheres of women's culture, causes the conservative narrative to recede, and then, another narrative, which seems to have disappeared and lost its voice, comes forth and speaks up. Such listening, causes silence to speak, in Showalter's words.

This model of a dual feminine voice was also adopted by Van Dijk-Hemmes and Athalya Brenner,[7] who examined the possibility that some of the biblical stories were written by female authors, rather than male ones. They argued that the canonical stories should be examined as having twofold voices, and as gender-dependent texts, and that one should seek the blurred, erased or encrypted layer, which speaks from the sphere of women's culture and from the expanses of the authentic female being and experience.

5. Gilbert and Gubar, *The Mad Woman in the Attic*; Rich, "When We Dead Awaken"; Keren, Like a Sheet in the Hand of the Embroideress.
6. Showalter, "Feminist Criticism in the Wilderness," 243–70.
7. Van Dijk-Hemmes and Brenner, *On Gendering Texts*.

Another important step in the process of uncovering the censored female story, is the study of the biblical stories in a way that is connected to the culture of the ancient Near East, while being aware of its symbols, rituals and customs. The ancient religion of Israel was not created ex nihilo. While biblical editors and post-biblical interpreters have tried to produce and provide the biblical scriptures and the life of faith with a character that presumes to be separated from the Canaanite culture, the truth is that the biblical figures lived within the Canaanite world, drawing from, and merging with it. The religions of the region, as well as the Mesopotamian and Egyptian cultures have greatly influenced the formation of Israel's religion, along with the culture and stories inherent in the people's heritage and history. Therefore, it is sometimes possible to reconstruct deleted plot segments, or to identify censored female rites or rituals, based on the understanding of the ancient perception and awareness of the symbolic meanings prevalent in the ancient world.

The recognition of the double female voice enables an encounter with the traditions of a trailblazing feminine world, which although ancient and millennia-old, is often radical and revolutionary in nature, even in terms of the enlightened world in the twenty-first century.

The first Wonder Woman was already portrayed, thousands of years before the present one, by the biblical Yael, who made it quite clear to the warrior and oppressor that a woman is capable of being as strong and fierce a warrior as he is, and she will subdue those who threaten her safety and security.

The origins of the revolutionary and defiant spirit that inspired the present-day #MeToo campaign can be traced back, quite surprisingly, to the midrashic character of Hannah the Maccabee. Hannah is the Jewish heroine of Hanukkah, who publicly asserts that she refuses to be an objectified, harassed and assaulted sex object. The androcentric social norm did permit this, but Hannah revolted and rose against these offensive edicts with all her might.

In light of the current battles of the lesbian, gay bisexual, transgender and queer or questioning (LGBTQ) community for

Preface

legitimization and recognition of non-heterosexual families, and considering the opposition of religious leaders in the name of the holy scriptures, the book of Ruth actually provides support and inspiration to the LGBTQ community. The story of Ruth and Naomi, which marks the cradle of King David's lineage, is in fact the subversive story of an alternative family. The two women, depicted as bound together with great love and devotion, raise Ruth's child as two mothers, while the father, Boaz, serves mainly as a sperm donor.

While in the current times of the 2020s, a female president or political leader is not commonplace, chapter 5 considers Miriam, the bold Prophetess who is Moses' oppositional leader. Moses is a charismatic leader but Miriam dares to challenge his autocracy and she charts a different path from the one that he outlined. Along with her, the mysterious figures of Pharaoh's daughter and Zipporah outline for us the possibility, and sometimes even the necessity of displaying a female-unique opposition and resistance to the patriarchal decree—be it the decree of God, the sovereign, the rabbi, the father or the husband.

Chapter 7 in the book will portray the story of Sarah, the first Matriarch. Sarah fights for the survival of the sacred heritage of motherhood and against the Patriarchy's violent acts of subjugation. Despite her absence from the overt story, from the moment of her son's binding, the chapter will describe her implicit presence, which is uncovered by deciphering the iconographic language of the ancient religions of Israel. This language recounts Israel's founding Mother's refusal to obey the patriarchal ethos of sacrifice. This maternal resistance stands as a poignant protest against the sanctification of the willingness to sacrifice the son in the name of religious megalomania.

Chapter 8 of this book will bring forward the spirited, provocative and uninhibited voice of the female protagonist of the "Song of Songs," which is daring and groundbreaking, and befits the voice of the sexually liberated women and sexuality in this present permissive era. Her text-sex speaks of active and boundless female passion and represents corporeal-sexual sovereignty free of all shame and guilt. This erotic, wild and fiery text, lying between the sacred pages of the Bible, is a defiant and bold response to the degradation and debasement of female sexuality in the patriarchal pornographic and violent descriptions, found in other parts of the Bible.

The exposure of the subversive, rebellious, and powerful aspects of the women of the Jewish tradition may give a corrective and restorative shape to the experience and sense of ostracism, diminution, and distortion that Adler has described. The traditional story, on its overt level, often erases and distorts the image of women and their world. However, at the covert and encrypted level, are teeming female voices, which have outlived the processes of blurring and deletion. The defiant meanings that were not allowed to be heard and could not culturally survive within patriarchal societies and times "went underground," under the supervising radar, thus surviving within the pages of the constitutive stories. They survived in order to be rediscovered and re-taught, to serve as a liberating anchor and a basis of power for female readers. Thus, they may also turn a spotlight and lead toward a path of liberation, as well as gender and personal empowerment, for the woman, who encounters the ancient stories of her religion with a renewed reading.

Chapter 1

Sexual Politics in the Biblical Narrative

> *The woman in my subtitle affirms her right to refuse the authority of the Bible, and the manipulations of the biblical narrator . . . To read as a woman means to practice a counter-reading that is made possible by a long familiarity with the status of the outsider. Reading as a woman means reading . . . as the reader refusing her position in the margins.*[1]

THE FEMININE CHARACTERS IN the Bible are generally portrayed as marginal in relation to the dominant male characters. There are various assumptions concerning the reasons for this biased presentation—one assumption is that the feminine voice was blurred and censored because it did not serve the androcentric interests of the patriarchy and the interests of the biblical author as the agent of the patriarchy. Another assumption is that positioning the feminine voice at the center did not comply with the sociocultural order prevailing at the time in which the traditions were documented or processed, and so, it was necessary to adapt the

---

1. Fuchs, *Sexual Politics in the Biblical Narrative*, 17.

traditions in the spirit of those generations, so that the spiritual guidance would be more welcomed and accepted.

However, researchers assume that popular female traditions, which depicted the biblical heroines as dominant and central, have subsisted in the past, but they were concealed since they denoted the central role of women in the spiritual, religious, social and cultural strongholds of ancient Israel. Some of these traditions have shed a critical light on male theology and its weaknesses. Therefore, silencing these traditions and concealing them both culturally and religiously have constituted a political act of shaping the heritage for future generations in accordance with the needs of the patriarchy.

The reconstruction of the silenced and concealed feminine story is inspired by critical literary research, which exposed the literary creative sphere as entailing power struggles, mechanisms of oppression and gender politics. The canonical text should be read critically to cast doubt on the reliability of the portrayal of feminine characters, while exposing the manipulation of denial and erasure embedded in it.

Feminist literary research shows that to fully uncover the female voice, through the mechanisms of diminution, oppression and reduction, the canonical texts must be read as gendered texts. Such a reading will be aware of the effect of gender, class and religious identity of the author/narrator documenting, on his decision on issues such as: what should be told, and what should be silenced, ignored and denied? Who is included in the story and who is excluded? What is told and what is ignored? Who is chosen to be remembered and mentioned and who should be forgotten? What is chosen to be sanctified and present, and what is chosen to be banished and degraded? Who is being exalted and glorified and who is diminished and reduced?[2]

The basic assumption of feminist literary research is that the authority of the author who holds the pen—an authority entrusted mainly to men—has led to almost total dominance of the patriarchal perception in shaping culture and religion. In their classic

---

2. Elior, Grandmother Didn't Know to Read and Write, 776.

book *Madwoman in the Attic* Gilbert and Gubar[3] described how male writers almost totally dominated the presentation of the characters of the women they wrote about. The male writers had an oppressive and repressive influence on female composition and feminine texts. Gilbert and Gubar argued that the writer's pen, is the instrument with which he creates worlds and engenders a textual universe. He functions as the representative of the omnipotent God—the creator of the universe and the owner of sovereignty and authority. The author, who pretends to be the representative of God, appropriates control over the characters and events, through control of the recording of the statements and the verses. The author is in fact, the founding father of the patriarchy, because he creates the faith of future generations with the help of his pen. He creates a world and system in the image of the patriarchy, according to its needs.

In this system, women are defined as an object that is subject to the patriarch's point of view and definition. Their characters are drawn by portrait lines that have been placed on them like a mask. Their points of view, experiences and world are defined and formulated by the point of view of the author and his male-centered perception. Women are mostly presented as lacking sovereignty over their bodies and lives, lacking authority and autonomy, unless they are granted a special authorization to take sovereignty over their lives. Their story is presented as marginal and relatively peripheral, and they operate like puppets on strings in the stories of the men.

Gilbert and Gubar argue that to uncover the authentic female story, the women should be extricated from the masks put on their figures and released from the mirror images that imprisoned them. To this end, the woman reader is required to venture and look behind the mirror—beyond the patriarchal definitions and stories.

Rich[4] continues this line of thought and explains the importance of revisionist reading—a critical reading that liberates the

---

3. Gilbert and Gubar, *The Mad Woman in the Attic*.
4. Rich, "When We Dead Awaken."

feminine text from its captivity. Such reading is a feminist survival act—it enables the expropriation of the values of hegemonic culture and their traditional accepted context, and the discovery of values and traditions that are true to women and their world, and that speak them and their lives. Inspired by Rich, Keren writes that a revisionist reading enables women to "adopt their own place on the world's cultural map that has excluded them to its margins."[5] This is, as Rich puts it, "the act of looking back, of seeing with fresh eyes, of entering an old text from a new critical direction."[6]

Reading the canonical text with subversive eyes and from a critical point of view that does not shy away from its traditional theological weight, is a reading that is aware of the manipulative mechanisms employed by the author. Prince[7] argues that the reader must be aware that the narrator is a character, who tries to seem to be a non-character—that is, he pretends to make his voice an omniscient voice, devoid of interests and loyal to an absolute truth, when in fact, it is not necessarily so. The narrator will try to entice the reader to believe that he is the sole and exclusive narrator, in order not to infringe on his exclusive authority. Chatman[8] points to the ways in which the author "plants" statements that render the reader neutralized of his critical thinking, thus illuminating the need to be a wary reader. Hochman[9] and Bal[10] point to the importance of the gaze that the narrator tries to control. The narrator directs the reader's gaze to a particular character, who is the protagonist or the main character, and neutralizes the gaze at other characters. Thus, he also lowers or neutralizes the voices and presence of these characters and amplifies the voice of the character he wishes to highlight above others. Therefore, the

---

5. Keren, *Like a Sheet in the Hand of the Embroideress*, 12.
6. Rich, "When We Dead Awaken," 18.
7. Prince, "Introduction to the Study of the Narratee," 7–25.
8. Chatman, *Story and Discourse*.
9. Hochman, *Character in Literature*.
10. Bal, *Narratology*.

woman critical reader must dare to "go beyond the ideology of the narrator"[11]—beyond his guidance, judgment and interests.

The woman reader, according to Bach,[12] must look beyond the narrator's gaze, suspect his credibility, and refuse to be an ideal and obedient reader. She must refuse to blindly accept the explanations and insights presented by the narrator, and she must look in the textual sphere for hints of what he did not want her to recognize or see. Regarding female characters in the Bible, Bach argues that the women are trapped in a story that is not theirs, collapsing under its crushing and silencing weight. Therefore, the reader, who refuses to be another crushed and obedient object, is required to release the fictitious character created by the patriarchal author, and to allow the authentic feminine image to be revealed and uncovered and to reveal at the same time, her story and heritage as well. Bach, inspired by Spivak[13] urges the woman reader not to be afraid to run with text and go somewhere else, beyond the narrator's intention. In this way she can identify, and see the spheres, in which women have been brushed away. When the reader challenges the omniscient narrator's voice, then—"the female character will not be in such danger of oozing away."[14]

11. Exum, "Second Thoughts About Secondary Characters," 79.
12. Bach, "Signs of the Flesh," 351–65.
13. Spivak and Rooney, "In a Word, Interview," 124–56, 145.
14. Bach, "Signs of the Flesh," 351.

Chapter 2

From an Angel to a Lethal Monster
Transformation and Subversion in the Story of Biblical Yael[1]

> "You [men] make the worlds wherein you move...
> Our world, and in its narrow confines, shut in
> four blank walls... we act our parts."[2]

THIS QUOTE, TAKEN FROM the classic book by Gilbert and Gubar,[3] illustrates the way in which women and mothers are culturally trapped within representations created by men, based on their needs and perceptions. Gilbert and Gubar portray the images of the angel and the monster as eternal images that preserve the woman between two poles: the containing, giving, soft and obedient woman-mother, who knows her place within the domestic sphere, and the woman-monster-witch, the rebellious, bold warrior, the one who undermines the patriarchal rules and regulations. This

---

1. First published in *Feminist Theology* 29.1 (2020).
2. A Woman's Poem, *Harper's Magazine* (February 1859) in Gilbert and Gubar, *The Mad Woman in the Attic*, 18.
3. Gilbert and Gubar, *The Mad Woman in the Attic*.

From an Angel to a Lethal Monster

division does not do justice to the more complex character of the woman, as she knows herself as a subject, and as women know themselves and their being.

In this chapter I will focus on the image of such a multifaceted woman from the biblical stories, who is portrayed as the associate of Deborah the Prophetess in saving the people of Israel—Yael, the wife of Heber the Kenite. Yael's story presents two faces that correspond to the mythical feminine images that Gilbert and Gubar present in their research—the caring, nourishing and enveloping woman-mother, and the diabolical, murderous, lethal and bold woman. I will explore these two faces and the transformative dynamics that generate the transition between them. The examination of these dynamics will be based on theories that focus on the female body as a political site through which the women's oppression, subjugation and disciplining are carried out. The theories that I present describe the restraining and stifling hold of the phallocentric and androcentric order over the body of the female angel figure. At the same time, they depict the body also as an oppositional force, through and in which a radical and defiant action takes place, spurning the image of the maternal angel, to extricate oneself from that overpowering grip. This will be illustrated in Yael's story as an act that protests not only against the act of rape carried out by the male enemy army, but also against the male culture of rape.

Two Mythical Feminine Poles in the Patriarchal Literature

In their classic book *Madwoman in the Attic* Gilbert and Gubar portray the creative woman, as imprisoned in mythical masks put on her face by the patriarch—the person of authority holding the pen. These masks represent two poles of eternal feminine types that fulfill the androcentric need. This dichotomous division enhances the male ownership of women and femininity.

The one eternal type described by the researchers is the "angel"—the pure, humble, gentle, passive woman, the enveloping, submissive, docile, caring, healing, nurturing, devoted mother, who provides advice and comfort to others, and who cares first and foremost, for her household members. The image of the angel, or more precisely, "the angel in the house," is based on Virginia Woolf's observation, that the woman is identified with the domestic-family sphere, which she is expected to serve. As the angel in the house, her submissiveness and passiveness allow the man to feel superior and of value. The woman, as an angel, reflects for the man his double and enlarged image, which means that she serves as a "pleasing looking glass."[4] It is her consent to be and exist as reduced and lessened that enables him to become stronger. Gilbert and Gubar continue this analysis of the image of the woman as an angel, claiming that it reflects an ideal of purity and selfless observation, to the extent that she lacks selfhood. A woman-angel relinquishes her selfhood when she agrees to subsist with no significant action in the world. She lives without a story of her own, and her sole role is to support his (the man's) story—his desires and aspirations. All she wishes is to please the man, and her virtues depend on the extent of her submission to his will. The woman-angel is enclosed in the temple of her home, and she functions as the safe haven, city of refuge and as the "horns of the altar" for the man, who flees to her warm bosom, escaping from the blood and sweat that accompany the life of significant action in the world.

The other eternal type is the "monster" or the witch. The woman-monster is portrayed as evil and destructive and is characterized by uncompromising personal autonomy. She is opinionated, demands power and control, places her desires and wishes in first priority, and maneuvers her surroundings to fulfill her needs and objectives. She has powerful and dangerous talents. Her character refuses to remain in the place designated by the patriarchal text, and she writes her own text, not renouncing her own story.

Going back to Woolf's depiction of the angel of the house, then the monster is the woman who refuses to be another pleasing looking glass for the man. She no longer allows her self-reduction for his intensification. "For if she begins to tell the truth, the figure

---

4. Woolf, *A Room of One's Own*, 45.

From an Angel to a Lethal Monster

in the looking glass shrinks"; Woolf writes.[5] The very refusal of the woman to erase her selfhood is a threat to the man's self-esteem and status, and she, therefore, becomes the symbol of all that is evil and diabolical.

The two images—the angel and the monster—are indeed opposing and even polarized, but in fact, as shown by Gilbert and Gubar, they are also interrelated. The woman-angel contains an intrinsic paradox—she is so pure and chaste that she cannot be tangible and substantial. She is distanced from any reality or selfhood. She is so self-alienated that the power of selfhood within her cannot remain silent any longer, if she wants to stay alive. Within the frail selfless woman, the hidden desire for power awakens, and when it succeeds in permeating and erupting, it also ignites a deadly potential against those who try to limit her steps and block her expressions. The woman imprisoned inside the figure of the angel may, therefore, be filled with a yearning to escape. She has the dangerous (for the patriarch) capability to erupt in a rising fury.

The two images of the woman described by the researchers contain a paralyzing message in the patriarchal world—either the woman lives a life of silence and submission (the angel), or she must be silenced and defeated (the monster). That is to say, either the woman exists as a selfless being, of her own so-called free will and choice, or she will be subjected to paralyzing and oppressive practices that will force her to give up on herself. This is the deadly glass coffin in which women are trapped in the patriarchal texts, as they do not allow feminine subjectivity to fulfill itself as it is, with all its complexity and full humanity. Thus, her vision, her self-development and choices are distorted. To release herself from this coffin, the woman is required to shed the dead and false self. She must identify the true self on her own, beyond all the transcriptions and patterns that were made for her, and she must dare to embrace practices of freedom,[6] sovereignty and authority.

---

5. Woolf, *A Room of One's Own*, 46.

6. Virginia Woolf referred to the habits of freedom that the creative woman must adopt to free herself from the boundaries of the family room that limits her thinking, daring and creativity. Woolf, *A Room of One's Own*, 125.

Awake, Awake

Yael—Between an Angel and a Monster

> Howbeit Sisera fled away on his feet to the tent of Jael the wife of Heber the Kenite; for there was peace between Jabin the king of Hazor and the house of Heber the Kenite. And Jael went out to meet Sisera, and said unto him: 'Turn in, my lord, turn in to me; fear not.' And he turned in unto her into the tent, and she covered him with a rug. And he said unto her: 'Give me, I pray thee, a little water to drink; for I am thirsty.' And she opened a bottle of milk, and gave him drink, and covered him (Judg 4:17–19).

If we examine the character of Yael in the biblical story (Judg 4) and in the song of Deborah (Judg 5), which adds more details about Yael's actions with Sisera, then we can clearly see how at the beginning of the story Yael appears as the typical "woman—angel" character. She is maternal and devoted, compassionate, giving, caring and enveloping. Yael is defined and characterized by the text as a housewife—one that dwells in her tent. In chapter 4, she is described as moving around her tent and working in it, and in chapter 5, Deborah describes her as the woman of the tent, when she sings—"above women in the tent shall she be blessed."(5:24). Yael, therefore, corresponds to the image of "angel of the house," as dubbed by Woolf, and as described by Gilbert and Gubar. She is described as a housewife, who comes out of her tent to greet the fleeing warlord and offer him shelter and cover. She functions like the typical angel figure, as a kind, gracious and merciful hostess. She offers the character of the male hero the opportunity to hold on to her and to the warm home she offers, as the "horns of the altar"—a safe and comforting refuge from the results of his dramatic and bloody activity on the battlefield.

Until this point, Yael is the woman, who has no story of her own, but works for **his** (man's) story and supports his action. In addition, as a typical mother-angel, she is nourishing, soft and enveloping, and offers Sisera a warm blanket and comforting milk, as a mother offers and provides to her nursing baby.

From an Angel to a Lethal Monster

From this point there is ambiguity in the text regarding what transpired between Yael and Sisera. In the account of events in chapter 4 there is no hint of a sexual incident, but in the Song of Deborah, in chapter 5, a clear hint is presented when Deborah sings: "At her feet he sunk, he fell, he lay; at her feet he sunk, he fell; where he sunk, there he fell down dead" (5:27). In the Hebrew version it explicitly says that he *fell between her legs*. In other words, Deborah clearly implies a sexual encounter. Considering this statement, the researchers express conflicting views regarding the existence of sexual intercourse between Yael and Sisera. Stocker[7] explicitly argues that Sisera raped Yael, but on the other hand, Bal[8] believes that she slept with him voluntarily, and was not raped. Bal explains that Yael probably had sexual relations with Sisera, so that she could weaken and overpower him later. Shemesh,[9] on the other hand, believes that there is no basis for assuming that there was sexual intercourse between Yael and Sisera. She argues that the erotic clues are designed to ridicule the enemy's expectations and to accentuate its failure and defeat. Shemesh refers to the maternal clues at the beginning of Yael's story as nullifying the assumption of sexual relations between her and Sisera. She argues that the signs that were interpreted as sexual are in fact an extension of the maternal imagery, and the Hebrew expression "between her legs" or "at her feet he sunk," which Deborah uses in her song, links to the circumstances in which a baby is born between his mother's legs. In the situation in question, Sisera, who relies on Yael's help as a protective mother figure while being helpless and weak as a baby born between his mother's legs, suddenly finds himself attacked by her.

Nevertheless, in relating to Deborah's problematic statements, Shemesh[10] regards the story of Judith, which was not included in the canonical tradition, as a purifying and amending mirror story to the story of Yael. In the book "Judith," the heroine is described as performing a seduction scene for the enemy, whom she later

---

7. Stocker, *Judith–Sexual Warrior*.
8. Bal, *Death and Dissymmetry*.
9. Shemesh, "'Yet he Committed No Act of Sin with Me,'" 159–77.
10. Shemesh, "'Yet he Committed No Act of Sin with Me,'" 159–77.

slays, but the narrator stresses that she did not intend to have intercourse with the man and that no sexual contact took place. This is why it says in the book of Judith: "and the Lord hath not suffered me his handmaid to be defiled, but hath brought me back to you without pollution of sin," (13:20). In this way, the version in the book of Judith clears the image of the most lethal heroine of all suspicion of sexual promiscuity, impurity or disgrace.

Despite these arguments, I would like to point out additional clues and ambiguities in the text that reinforce the assumption that the scene between Yael and Sisera did include an encounter of a sexual nature. In addition to the very clear-cut insinuation to Yael's female genitalia ("between her legs," in the Hebrew version), Deborah also notes in her song: "where he sunk, there he fell down dead" (5:27). There are various interpretations of this description. However, I would like to propose another interpretation of this verse, which relates to the structure of the verse as a description of cause and effect—Sisera sank between Yael's legs, that is, he bent over her as he tried to rape her, and that is why he also fell and was overpowered by her. Deborah, according to this argument, describes Yael's rape or attempted rape, and thus she reveals what the biblical narrator tried to obscure, erase or conceal. Deborah's song, therefore, does not let us repress or forget, and the allusions to the sexual-aggressive event resonate as opposed to, and despite the silencing attempts.

The assumption presented here that the Song of Deborah speaks the silence of the act of rape, is based, among other things, on the fact that it speaks of the silence and marginality of other feminine experiences. Lederman-Daniely writes as follows in her study of the Song of Deborah:

Deborah places the mother center stage, even when referring to the mother of the enemy. Her song relates to female experiences that are "blind spots" in the male definition of culture and experience. She speaks of the mother's agonizing wait for her son to return from war and the practice of raping women as a customary cruel, violent and demeaning act of male conquest. Her description of the weeping mother of Sisera waiting for her son, and the explanations of her maids that he is late because he is busy in raping the wombs of the conquered women, were interpreted as a song of derision and mockery of the enemy, yet Dijk-Hemmes and Brenner,[11] have proposed a different approach. They argue that the hegemonic text should be read as a text with a double voice—one voice is an obedient voice that is consistent with the prevailing ideology, and the other is a subversive feminine voice, encrypted and hidden from the eye. The tone of mockery of Sisera, then, may be revealed as a harsh criticism not only of the man from the enemy army, but also of the male culture of war and rape.[12]

The tone of derision, according to Lederman-Daniely, functions as the obedient veil consistent with the male order, which enables the encryption of feminine criticism on a more concealed level. And so, if the Song of Deborah exposes silenced feminine experiences while expressing an encrypted criticism, one can also consider the verse: "At her feet (between her legs) he sunk, he fell, he lay; at her feet he sunk, he fell; where he sunk, there he fell down dead" (5:27), as a description of an act of rape, which was blurred and obscured by the author of chapter 4. In addition, the very information that Deborah adds that Sisera was infamous for raping the wombs of the women he conquered, as this was his common practice, reinforces the hypothesis that as a serial rapist, he also tried to rape Yael.

Another clue to the act of rape may be found in verse 21 in chapter 4. In the description of the killing of Sisera, it reads: "Then Jael Heber's wife took a tent-pin, and took a hammer in her hand, and went softly unto him, and smote the pin into his temples, and it pierced through into the ground; for he was in a deep sleep; so he swooned and died." When examining the actions described in the verse, one can detect a confused order of actions, which is not necessarily consistent or logical—If the first action performed was the insertion of the peg into his temple, how did Sisera fall asleep following it, and then he was tired, and only then did he die? The lack of logic in the order of actions may indicate an attempt to

---

11. Van Dijk-Hemmes and Brenner, *On Gendering Texts*.
12. Lederman-Daniely, "I Arose a Mother in Israel," 19–20.

Awake, Awake

obscure and re-edit an ancient tradition that told a different story than the one told by the later edited tradition.

It is possible that the ancient tradition told of rape, and the description of "into the ground" describes not Sisera's temple, but Yael, who was thrown to the ground while being assaulted and raped. After this sexual activity, Sisera apparently got tired and fell asleep, and then, Yael retaliated with a parallel rape, by inserting the peg into his temple and killing him.[13] This hypothesis, regarding the revision of ancient tradition, is reinforced by Zackovitch's argument.[14] Zakovitch, who examined this scene, argued that the differences between the Song of Deborah (chapter 5) and the description of the killing of Sisera in chapter 4, stem from the later processing of an ancient tradition. According to the older version, Sisera died in Yael's bed, but to defend both Yael and God's honor, the ancient tradition was clouded and re-edited as the known version that appears in chapter 4.

If we go back to the analysis of Yael's character according to eternal feminine images that were presented in the beginning, then at this stage of events, Sisera, as well as the readers, discover that Yael, who matched the image of the angel-woman lacking a "story of her own," is not necessarily so. In her decision to act against Sisera, Yael transforms and suddenly becomes a key figure in the plot of heroism and salvation. She becomes a major factor that defeats the enemy's warlord. In the face of the woman reader, Yael removes the mask of the mother-angel and puts on the mask of the lethal monster.

This raises the question: what makes Yael turn from a compassionate woman into a cruel and violent warrior? Is it possible, that beforehand she had planned to strike and defeat the warlord, that is, she was "a monster" from the outset, in both her personality and character?

---

13. Reference to the description of Sisera's murder as a reversed rape can be found, among others, in Ashman, "Women in the Bible as Victims of War," 169–83.

14. Zakovitch, "Sissera's Tod," 364–74.

From an Angel to a Lethal Monster

Indeed Sivan[15] argues that portraying Yael as a compassionate caregiver was in fact a misleading move, and from the very beginning, her behavior as a gracious hostess, gives a clue regarding the adoption of masculine patterns of hospitality that do not conform to accepted "coy" feminine patterns. However, the character evidence provided by Deborah regarding Yael's personality may negate this assumption. Deborah claims in her song that "Blessed above women shall Jael be, the wife of Heber the Kenite, above women in the tent shall she be blessed" (Judg 5:24). Yael is blessed among all women as a woman in the tent—that is, as a woman in her home. So, according to Deborah's testimony, Yael is a loyal housewife, and not (at least not from the outset) a warrior and a murderer. This is also evident from the weapon she used—she did not carry a knife or any other weapon, but used what was at her disposal, apparently in a spontaneous and unplanned moment—the tent peg.

What, then, created the revolutionary transformation in her character, from a woman-angel in her tent to a lethal and fearless murderer?

From a Subjugating and Domineering Trauma to Expressions of Courage and Subversion

> In the beginning, if there ever was such a time, Demeter, the goddess of life, gave birth to four daughters named Persephone, Psyche, Athena and Artemis. The world's first children were unremarkably happy ... A chariot thundered, then clattered into their midst. It was Hades, the middle aged god of death, come to rape Persephone ... come to commit the first act of violence earth's children had ever known ... What has become of Persephone and Psyche ... ? They became Cinderella, Snow White and Sleeping Beauty, whom Demeter, in the form of stepmother, sentenced to be trained and dumb.[16]

---

15. Sivan, *Between Woman, Man and God*.
16. Chesler, *Women and Madness*.

Awake, Awake

As portrayed by the researcher and psychologist Phyllis Chesler, rape and sexual abuse in the ancient mythology are mutilating, oppressive, offensive, subjugating and weakening elements in women's lives—both in ancient times and throughout the ages. Herman[17] in her constitutive book *Trauma and Recovery*, and Wolf[18] in her revolutionary book on female sexuality, depict findings that attest to the devastation caused to the soul, spirit and even the biology and neurology of the woman because of rape and sexual assault. Long-term sexual oppression undermines the very being and existence of the woman, argue Dworkin[19] and MacKinnon:[20]

> when you are objectified sexually, your being is enforced by a social meaning that defines you as an object for sexual use, according to the uses that are required of you... The mechanism employed in sex is power, which is imbued with significance, since it is the means of death, and death is... the ultimate transformation of a person into object.[21]

Similarly, Irigaray described the female body as an "object machine" and the bodies of women as "flying and raped" The body exists as distorted and alienated to itself in the patriarchal system and framework. She writes:

> You try to conform to an alien order. Exiled from yourself, you fuse with everything you meet... You become whatever touches you. In your eagerness to find yourself again, you move indefinitely far from yourself... passing from master to master, changing face, form, and language with each new power that dominates you. You-we are sundered.[22]

---

17. Herman, *Trauma and Recovery*.
18. Wolf, *Vagina*.
19. Dworkin, *Intercourse*.
20. MacKinnon, "Sexuality, Pornography and Method," 376–415.
21. MacKinnon, "Sexuality, Pornography and Method."
22. Irigaray, *This Sex Which Is Not One*, 200, 71.

From an Angel to a Lethal Monster

These descriptions spell out the extent to which the female body is vulnerable to the processes of weakening and subordination under the hegemonic system. However, the female body is also a source of defiant power, as well as the basis of the forces of formation, rehabilitation and rebirth. Cixous,[23] for example, identified in the corporeal-feminine sphere rebellious and subversive forces that have the potential for healing and liberation from the toxic substances of oppression. She points to the instinctive and creative expression that stems from the feminine corporeal self, as connecting the woman to boldness that is breaking boundaries and guiding her toward the violation of the regimenting law of the patriarchy. In her essay "The Laugh of the Medusa," Cixous describes a physical-mental dimension that opposes its taming and restraining and devotes itself to its rebellious rage. When this power of selfhood awakens within the woman, she will do anything and everything to liberate her "immense chained physical territories...."[24] From these wild dynamics, the woman will strive to regain and appropriate the right to speak, and to revive her text to life—that is, the physical-instinctive and creative voice that lives within her and flows from her.

Inspired by Cixous, Halpern[25] also argues that the female body manifests, in certain extreme situations, a rebellious, revolutionary and defying display. She presents in her study, through an analysis of literary texts, the ways in which the body strives to express the possibilities of feminine identity that have been censored and silenced in the male culture. She illustrates how the body, which has been taught to be a passive material, manifests in certain situations, an active display of heresy and defiance, and breaches in various ways its policing and restraining mechanisms. In other words, the feminine body is not only text that was written and enforced by the system, but it also writes the rebellion against the system.

---

23. Cixous, "The Laugh of the Medusa," 134–54.
24. Cixous, "The Laugh of the Medusa," 139.
25. Halpern, *Discontent Body*.

Lederman-Daniely[26] has written along the same lines, when pointing out the need to relate to the physical dimension in a discussion about a liberating feminine theology: "the female organs are not only a pleasant cushion to cuddle up in, a breast to nourish from and a containing womb to grow in, but they are the symbols of the female authenticity and the female source. They are her power, the self that will not give up on itself, and the urge to rebel against anything that threatens to eliminate, erase, or silence her self."

Considering this it can be construed that the feminine corporeal-mental experience, which is generally perceived as associated with the angelic-maternal aspects that envelop and nourish the other, is not necessarily merely that. From this experience the monstrous power can also flow—a resistant force that fights for the might of its vitality, resources and possibilities.

Going back to Gilbert and Gubar's arguments concerning the female mythic archetypes, then their claim that the angel and the monster are not that disconnected from each other, is reinforced by the observations of the presented theorists. When the woman-angel becomes estranged from herself to the point of fading and even death of her selfhood and being, her force of selfhood may struggle for its survival and rise with all its might. When the rage over the silencing overflows within the weakened, devoid woman, a subversive potential that Gilbert and Gubar named the "demonic yearning to escape," arises in her body.[27]

This demonic yearning, which is evident in bodily actions and expressions that disrupt the normative order, is often attributed to the areas of feminine insanity. Bordo[28] and Chesler argue that madness, lunacy and abnormality among women indicate the violence and oppression that were exerted on the woman. Madness is a political act and the only way of the female voice-body, which is silenced and erased in a patriarchal society, to voice and express itself. The display of madness expresses a protest and a rejection of the oppressive actions of the order. A similar position is expressed

26. Lederman-Daniely, "From Your Blood You Will See God," 13.
27. Gilbert and Gubar, *The Mad Woman in the Attic*, 26.
28. Bordo, *Unbearable Weight*.

From an Angel to a Lethal Monster

by Adler,[29] who viewed women's perverse and criminal behavior and the breach of the normative order, as a sign of an attempt to liberate themselves from being traditionally tamed.

If we return to Yael's story, then it is possible to detect "manifestations of insanity" expressed through the actions of her body. These expressions of insanity represent a battlefield of conflicting ideologies and forces.

The tent-home of a woman, like her body, is a site where she undergoes a process of regimenting and disciplining in a patriarchal society. She is restricted to domestic activity, and is ordered to serve, with her bodily actions, the needs of the patriarch and patriarchy. Yael, as a housewife, a woman who dwells in her tent, as depicted by Deborah, implements and expresses a text written for her—a text imposed upon her and her body, stifling and silencing many parts of her selfhood. Yet, and perhaps because of this, her story and actions are not limited only to the repressive text written for her, and her story reveals that her body also writes a text of protest.

Yael transforms the actions of her body from an obedient, submissive, serving and victim-like action toward Sisera, into a belligerent, vengeful, lethal and subversive action. From a victim of rape, she becomes a rapist, as she inserts her tent's peg into Sisera's temple. It is not only Sisera, as a patriarch, who pierces and scorches the violent culture of rape within her, but it is also her, who pierces and scorches a violent and lethal act of penetration into him in response.

If in the Song of Deborah, we read the description of Yael inserting the peg in light of the ideas that were presented, we will identify this description as embodying an oppositional practice and a subversive display of abjection:

> Her hand she put to the tent-pin, and her right hand to the workman's hammer; and with the hammer she smote Sisera, she smote through his head, yea, she pierced and struck through his temples. At her feet he sunk, he fell, he lay; at her feet he sunk, he fell; where he sunk, there he fell down dead. (Judg 5:26–27).

---

29. Adler, *Sisters in Crime*.

Awake, Awake

Deborah chooses to elaborate on the description of the murder, repeating again and again the portrayal of the striking and pounding on Sisera's head, and the description of the crushing and smashing of the skull between Yael's legs. This performance pounds and strikes the reader—the female blood that flows between Yael's legs (whether as a menstrual blood or as a bleeding wound following the rape) mixes and blends with his blood, skull, and even the brain fluid of the man, the warlord, who came to rape, and was penetrated and raped himself.

The display of killing created by Yael in her actions and by Deborah in her opulent and subversive poetics, is wild, menacing and monstrous. The image of the "monster"—the woman possessed by madness incessantly pounding on the temple of the warlord, crushing his head to the death, is, as we understand, an enraged extreme response to an institutionalized and severe repressive action. From the experience of rape, the defiant disruption of the mother-angel figure emerges. The compassionate and enveloping tent woman becomes a murderous woman. The tent peg—the basis of the house—turns into a lethal, bloody weapon in Yael's avenging hands.

And so, Yael's biblical story, and especially that reflected in the Song of Deborah, illustrates how the sites of the female regimentation—the home and the body—may undergo extreme transformation, following oppression and trauma, and become a rebellious site of bold, furious and vengeful decision. This transformative process spurns petrifying and oppressive feminine identities and produces a liberating and charging response, stemming from the core substances of the female entity.

Summary

"The stories of women slaying the enemy hero are written from a male perspective. Stories from this perspective bear no reference to any representation of the women's anxiety of the threatening status of being raped, however, the focus on the silenced perspective of the women may

From an Angel to a Lethal Monster

> reveal a different story. It is possible that these women murder men not only to save their people but also because they know that they face a particularly cruel equation. The victory of the enemy signifies rape and sexual violence toward them, or toward their daughters. The elimination of the hero turns the enemy into a passive object and thwarts the custom of turning the woman into a rape victim. In this radical act, they change the reality imposed on them."[30]

In these words, Ashman, who studied the weakened state of women in biblical wars, points to the absent feminine angle and the silenced feminine experience in the canonical text, when it comes to the rape of women as a customary act during wars. This chapter strove to further illuminate the feminine perspective in the story of biblical Yael. Considering the insights presented, this story emerges, along with being a canonical story of salvation, as an antithetical story of the hegemonic spirit—as one that fulfills a subversive and rebellious oppositional practice. The story of Yael was accepted in the Israeli tradition as a patriarchal text that presents the saving of the people of Israel during the period of Deborah. But, when the dutiful veil—according to which a foreign woman chooses to cooperate with the leaders of the people of Israel in their struggle against their enemies—is removed, another story resurfaces. This additional story represents a female voice, defying gender-class obedience and the offensive and repressive masculine order.

This subversive significance attributed to Yael's actions fits well with the gender wise subversive theme, which appears in the Song of Deborah. Lederman-Daniely has illustrated that apart from the fact that the Song of Deborah is a song of praise to the warriors and the victors in the war, it positions, at the same time, in the biblical center stage the image of the mother and her unique experiences. Deborah's song of praise is in effect a double feminine text—it seems to obey the patriarchal order of the Father, but it reveals the silenced voice of the woman-mother. It sounds like a

---

30. Ashman, "Women in the Bible as Victims of War," 169–83.

Awake, Awake

mockery of the enemy warlord, who planned to rape the women of Israel, but as previously argued, it scorches the hegemonic text with a sharp and piercing indictment against the male culture of rape. This indictment also goes to the ruling phase and the fatal verdict in Yael's story, which, as described, continues to intertwine a double narrative thread and integrates the textual "weaving" that Deborah spins.

This double textual weave or poetic work is assigned a vast cultural and spiritual significance, when its weaver is such an influential and eminent prophetess in the tradition and heritage of Israel. Keren,[31] in her study of the way in which the feminine text survives as a woven code encrypted into the regulating hegemonic text, refers to the importance of the code inherent in the text of the female soothsayer. This woman operates as a great and wise mother in ancient literature, and her artistic creation represents and symbolizes her mission as a corrective, restorative and healing figure. Deborah in her role as the prophetess of the nation, that is, as the great and wise woman-mother, clearly proclaims that she is the mother who arose to restore her people: "That thou didst arise a mother in Israel" (5:7). As a restorative national mother, she announces in the same breath that Yael is blessed above women. Yael, as illustrated, demonstrates in her choices and story the transformation of the obedient and passive woman-angel figure into a fighting and rebellious "monster." She represents the revolutionary transformative process undergone by a woman from a situation in which she silently accepts her fate, remaining without a story of her own, into a state in which she spurns the patriarchal mechanisms of submission and assumes sovereignty over her story and body. If, in doing so, she is crowned by the wise prophetess as "blessed above women," then, there is a revolutionary and liberating message here. The code of the weave-poem-song that she encrypts under the supervising radar of the patriarchy guides the women listeners and readers to dare to choose such a transformative action. By praising Yael's character and story, she points to the possibility of turning the subservience of the victim into an

---

31. Keren, *Like a Sheet in the Hand of the Embroideress.*

assaulting force.³² In this process, Deborah facilitates the restoration and healing of the body and soul of the women, who turn from victims—torn and subjugated—into heroines who regain their selfhood and the sovereignty over their bodies and their lives.

> Then she set out with the moon as her guide, in order to found a city, or rather a tribe, or even a culture, the likes of which the world had never known, in which every woman was a soldier and a mother, tears were as common as physical heroism, marriages considered despicable, and rape—something quite inconceivable.³³

---

32. The subversion of this message should not be underestimated, especially when it is enacted in the male canonical text. Opposition to the role of the mother-angel is one of the most threatening actions on patriarchy and its agents–"Only when we understand how much she has offered him, can we understand how much she disappointed him," Gottlieb says (Gottlieb, "Three Mothers," 194). With regard to this menacing disappointment, Rich pointed to the patriarch's horror at the possibility that compassion, and the maternal nourishing cloak would be denied of him, Rich, *Of Woman Born*.

33. Chesler, *Women and Madness* 15.

Chapter 3

Hanna the Maccabee

A Healing and Restorative Memory of Biblical Esther's Sexual Abuse

THE BOOK OF ESTHER, read on the holiday of Purim, has received many feminist research interpretations because it is a woman, Queen Esther, who is the heroine of the Book, and ultimately also the savior of the Jewish people. At the same time, the story of the banished Queen Vashti also portrays a subversive behavior of a queen, who insists on disobeying King Ahasuerus, refusing to serve as an object that he can flaunt and display.

Still, one cannot ignore the fact that Esther, the young virgin girl, is handed over to the king's harem to be used sexually. She is required to obey and fulfill his desires and urges, and is so obediently sacrificed by Mordecai, her uncle. Esther's body becomes a commodity in Mordecai's hands, enabling him to attain a higher position, closer to the king, and is a commodity in the hands of the people for the purpose of their salvation. Therefore, although parts of the book may serve as a liberating inspiration for women, other parts, and perhaps the most crucial ones, provide an oppressive and offensive tradition—a national memory that presents the female body as a manipulated object and as a commodity being exploited.

Hanna the Maccabee

On the other hand, the Midrash of another Jewish holiday of salvation—the Jewish holiday of Hanukkah—which unlike Esther's story was not included in the biblical canon, provides a national memory that reverses the tradition of sexual abuse that appears in the book of Esther. This reverse tradition is embodied in the Midrash of Hannah the Maccabee who is, at least according to one version of the midrash, the sister of the Maccabees, the famous heroes of Hanukkah.

This chapter presents the tradition of Hannah the Maccabee as responding to and debating with the book of Esther. I will illustrate how this midrash is a heroic, restorative and subversive version of the version of sexual obedience represented by Esther. The virgin girl, Hannah, unlike Esther, fights against the wish to peddle her for the needs of the people and for the needs of the men that are her patrons. As such, the neglected tradition of Hannah the Maccabee provides a tremendous potential of feminine liberation, empowerment, and healing from the painful and downtrodden traumatic history of sexual oppression and silencing for generations.

As researchers illustrate, the beginning of the book of Esther positions gender as a clear-cut class-hierarchical issue that runs through the Book, as the story unfolds. The description of abundance in the king's feast shows the wealth that is reserved for the men of the kingdom. And so, the description of the king's banquet is extensively rich in detail compared to the scarcity of the almost nonexistent description of the queen's feast. The reader is directed toward a patriarchal and androcentric standpoint.[1]

When ordered by the king, Queen Vashti is expected to arrive immediately, even though she is hosting a banquet at the same time. Her feast is marginal and immaterial compared to the king's feast. The attitude to Queen Vashti is merely to see her as an object that the king wants to parade around, show off and boast of as a property, an asset that epitomizes his honor

Queen Vashti's story emphasizes how feminine obedience, especially obedience relating to the female body, is perceived as

---

1. Bach, *Women, Seduction and Betrayal in Biblical Narrative*, 195.

critical and essential to the establishment and preservation of the patriarchal order. Vashti's refusal to appear and to parade herself in accordance with the needs and desires of the king, is experienced as a complete and explosive menace to his regime, and to the act of regimenting women to the desires of men:

> "And Memucan answered before the king and the princes: 'Vashti the queen hath not done wrong to the king only, but also to all the princes, and to all the peoples, that are in all the provinces of the king Ahasuerus. For this deed of the queen will come abroad unto all women, to make their husbands contemptible in their eyes, when it will be said: The king Ahasuerus commanded Vashti the queen to be brought in before him, but she came not" (Esth 1:17–18) . . .

> "for he sent letters into all the king's provinces, into every province according to the writing thereof, and to every people after their language, that every man should bear rule in his own house, and speak according to the language of his people." (Esth 1:22).

Based on the words of the king's adviser one can understand that there is a constant fear among the guardians and agents of the order, that the wife will not be under the control of the husband—not only in the palace but in the entire kingdom. In other words, the male's domination over his wife is at the basis of the social order and at the basis of the social power of the men in general, and of the king. Therefore the king accepts the advice of the counselor, and so the decree—"every man should bear rule in his own house,"—i.e., that every husband will control his wife—is sent to all the nations of the kingdom.

King Ahasuerus' decree that "every man should bear rule in his own house" reverberates intertextually to the text of Genesis, where it reads: "and thy desire shall be to thy husband, and he shall rule over thee" (Gen 3:16). This reverberation suggests how from the patriarchal standpoint, the motif of the husband's rule over his wife is fundamental in establishing the order of the world. The rulership and domination of the husband over his wife are perceived as part of a true and proper divine order, at least according to Gen 1.

Moreover, in the book of Esther, male domination over the wife, as well as the wife's obedience to her husband, are perceived as the foundations of men's hegemonic status. Women's disobedience might lead to the collapse of the order and disgrace to the king. This element of preserving feminine inferiority for the sake of glorifying masculinity is a common concept, found in the writings of Virginia Woolf and Simone de Beauvoir. Other feminist thinkers add the disciplining of the female body as an element of preserving female inferiority to validate the reign of the phallus in its symbolic and concrete domains. The fact that the woman's body is available and accessible to the husband, preserves the inferiority of the female to the supremacy of the phallus. Therefore, Vashti's refusal to be a female showcase object for the king, undermines the phallocentric, androcentric and symbolic order. A woman's sovereignty over her body, as demonstrated by Vashti, is a chaotic threat to the male regime. This explains the severe response—the replacement of the queen with "another that is better than she" (Esth 1:19). The better woman is of course, the one who will restore order, and will completely subject her body and wishes to the king's will and desires.

Although it seems that the plot of chapter 1 of the book of Esther is only an introduction that is not linked to the rest of the story, the other chapters were in fact, closely related to it at the time they were written. Chapter 1 still resonates as the events unfold and is present and influential over the issues that arise throughout the Book. Indeed, if the issue of dominance over women and their subjugation as the basis of the socio-cultural order is at the center of chapter 1, then this issue continues to accompany the story as a "quiet," silenced and yet thunderous background sound for a woman willing to confront the silent and traumatic levels that are reflected in it.

As the plot unfolds, it tells of sending Esther, the orphaned young girl, to Ahasuerus' harem. Mordecai, the adoptive parent of the abandoned child, the courageous man, who will later refuse to bow down to Haman and thus endanger the entire nation, does nothing to prevent the girl from being taken as a mistress to the king. Esther does whatever Mordecai commands her. In other words, she embodies the model desired by every man in the kingdom—a good and docile woman who does not dare to defy, refuse or raise doubts, who gives up her sovereignty over her body without a word.

When the death decree of the Jewish people is declared, Mordecai tears his clothes, puts on sackcloth with ashes and cries bitterly. At this point, he begins to activate Esther as a secret agent, and convinces her to go to the king and change the decree, despite the risk to her life. For Esther this is a turning point. She hesitates, realizes that she is endangering her life, but decides to act. She announces a national fast and then turns to Ahasuerus and succeeds in annulling the decree. She devises a rescue plan and becomes the leader of the battle, in which her people avenge on the people who wanted to kill them.

The book of Esther does not report of any distress associated with giving the young girl, Esther, to the king. The plight of young virgin girls, who are taken to the hegemonic ruler and raped by him was not perceived as an unusual issue to be dealt with, or as an issue that interferes with the flow of the story of heroism. No questions are raised regarding Mordecai's morality, as he abandons the girl for whom is responsible.

In fact, Esther's distress, as well as that of many girls in her position, is largely a silenced experience in biblical canonical literature. There is no one in the text to cry out the agony of the raped girl and recognize the trauma that this humiliating and offensive use generates within her.

Kehat[2] argues that these reactions of indifference and silencing are mostly typical also of the literary works of the Jewish Sages. The Sages are not aware of the plight and trauma of a raped woman. There is no awareness of her distress, and no proper response from the male society to the severity of the injury caused by rape, claims Kehat. She refers to issues discussed by the Torah sages and

2. Kehat, "The Cohen's Daughter," 103–7.

commentators and illustrates that the Sages found it difficult to view rape as a dangerous state to the woman. Therefore, if the ruler took her by force, she was still to be married at the time prescribed by the rabbis. Their deliberations unmistakably demonstrate a total absence of understanding of the horror experienced by a raped woman, to the extent that there is no halachic significance to this component in the face of the severity of changing a rabbinic ordinance.

The trauma caused by rape, is in effect, completely absent from the words, interpretations, questions and discussions of the Sages and commentators, and the rape itself is not considered as dangerous or being destructive and devastating to the woman's soul and wellbeing. Kehat argues that there is no recognition of the magnitude of the trauma, and there is a clear lack of awareness of the psychological damage resulting from the sexual abuse. This was the muted and silenced condition of women in the ancient cultures—no awareness of their suffering and pain because of rape. Kehat also notes that women who were raped were even accused of indifference and lack of emotion when raped and abused.

If we return to the book of Esther, then, as far as the sexual trauma experienced by the girl Esther in Ahasuerus' harem is concerned, this trauma is non-existent. Esther is silent about her terror and weakness. The only time Esther voices profound distress is her declaration of a national fast, before she enters to speak with the king, to annul the decree of annihilation of her people. Esther, at least according to the overt context, asks to fast for her sake, because she fears that she will be severely punished for initiating a conversation and appealing to the king without a prior invitation from him. It seems, at least according to the world of meanings of the hegemonic story, that she asks for the fast, as a spiritual act that will promote salvation from the decree of annihilation. Yet, the fact that Esther is forced to sexually please the king of whom she is terrified, to the point of fear of death and severe punishment, implies the depths of the sexual trauma, muted and hidden in the story.

And so, the sexual trauma experienced by Esther, remains a silenced event in the tradition of the canonical story of the Megillah. Still, in Jewish tradition there is another version of the story of handing the young girl to the ruler. This version clearly corresponds with the book of Esther. In this version, the sexual trauma bursts out of the silence in full force.

This narrative version is the midrash of Hannah the Maccabee. As I will explain, this traditional story gives center stage to the horror of rape, as well as to the feminine rage that arises considering the humiliation and debasement embodied in this act of sexual abuse.

Midrash of Hannah the Maccabee, as Speaking the Silence of Rape

In Jellinke's book, Beth ha-Midrasch, which features a collection of ancient rabbinic literature, there is the midrash of Hannah the Maccabee (or in another version, as the daughter of Yohanan), Which highlights a surprising, feminist and radical angle, in the story of the heroism of the traditional Hanukkah story.

The midrash, in its two known versions, tells the story of a young heroine who is supposed to be handed over for the ruler's sexual use. Her brother and father give her away without any protection or understanding of the severe injury about to be inflicted on her. The young woman is unwilling to be handed over. She undresses in public, thus raising the wrath of her brothers, who want to punish her and burn her at the stake. She explains the desperation of her actions, and the injustice of their actions, thereby persuading them to save her and go out to fight the oppressive ruler.

According to Kehat,[3] This midrash is revolutionary, first, because it sets the girl as the heroine of the salvation, and not the male warriors, as is customary in the Hanukkah tradition. She is the one described as setting off the rebellion and creating a conscious revolution—no longer surrender to injustice, humiliation and contempt, but rather opposition to oppression.

Furthermore, in the midrash we can identify descriptions giving a clear intertextual echo of the story of the book of Esther.

---

3. Kehat, "The Cohen's Daughter," 103–7.

Hanna the Maccabee

First, both stories depict a situation of obediently handing over a virgin girl to the ruler, when the male family members, who are supposed to protect the young woman (the brothers or the adoptive parent-uncle) allow this without comment or struggle. The midrash describes how Hannah's clothing is torn as an act of sorrow, fear and protest. This is analogous to the description of Mordecai's tearing his clothes in response to the decree of annihilation:

> "Now when Mordecai knew all that was done, Mordecai rent his clothes, and put on sackcloth with ashes, and went out into the midst of the city, and cried with a loud and a bitter cry" –Esth 4:1.

In fact, there is a parallel between the decree of the girl's rape and the decree of genocide. This is a subversive analogy because the rape of a girl, as described earlier, was not perceived as horrific or shocking in the hegemonic culture. It places the girl's rape as a true decree of annihilation to her heart and soul.

In addition, Hannah is dressed in royal garments as part of the trick that is played on the ruler, and Mordecai is described as wearing royal garments after Haman's scheme was foiled. Another little symbolic reverberation is the word "Hadasim" (myrtle) in the midrash, as "Hadasim" reverberates to Esther's second name, Hadassah.

Considering the intertextual echoes, the great differences between the two stories are blatant—Esther's silent obedience when taken to the king's harem for his sexual pleasure (Mordecai does not protect her or even try to prevent it. Maybe he even encourages it), as opposed to Hannah's fierce refusal and actions. If her father and brothers agree to her humiliation and debasement, she will certainly not allow it. The parallel between her actions to those of Mordecai only emphasizes the fact that she is doing what Mordecai did not do for Esther, for whom he was responsible. The analogy with Mordecai creates a gender reversal that is significant in presenting her power and boldness, which crosses common gender boundaries. This is a liberating reversal wherein the men display shameful cowardice—Mordecai in the case of handing

Esther over to Ahasuerus, and Hannah's brother in the case of handing her over to the ruler—Hannah rises and turns the tables. She bravely opposes her brother, crying out the cry of the raped and defiled woman.

It is noticeable that in her story, Esther is obediently dressing up and preparing herself for the time when the king decides to summon her and bed her– "that they may gather together all the fair young virgins unto Shushan the castle, to the house of the women, unto the custody of Hegai the king's chamberlain, keeper of the women; and let their ointments be given them; "(Esth 2:3). She remakes herself to be taken forcefully, as Dworkin[4] named it, despite the traumatic nature of this experience. Dworkin uses this expression in her radical book "Intercourse," when describing how the women's freedom in its deepest existential level is robbed through the act of male penetration: "Being female in this world means having been robbed of the potential for human choice."[5] In reference to preparing the body for intercourse, Dworkin writes: "One does not make choices in freedom. Instead, one conforms in body type and behavior and values to become an object of male sexual desire, which requires an abandonment of a wide-ranging capacity for choice . . . The surrender occurs before the act that is supposed to accomplish the surrender takes place . . . She has remade herself so as to prepare the way for the invasion of privacy that her preparation makes possible."[6]

An example of scandalous portrayal of the way a woman is educated to prepare herself for the sexual act, through which she relinquishes sovereignty over her body and freedom, appears in Pauline Reage's "Story of o." Reage[7] follows the process of sexualization and debauching of a woman and describes her preparation for the sexual usage: "Then I know that they untied the hands of o that were still tied behind her back, and they told her to undress, and they would bathe her and do her make up. They undressed her

---

4. Dworkin, *Intercourse*.
5. Dworkin, *Intercourse*, 54.
6. Dworkin, *Intercourse*, 54.
7. Reage, *Story of O*.

naked and put her clothes in the closets. They did not allow her to wash herself on her own and did her hair, as in a hairdressing salon..."[8]

This preparatory process is identical to the process of Esther's preparation, to be bedded by Ahasuerus: "Now when the turn of every maiden was come to go in to king Ahasuerus, after that it had been done to her according to the law for the women, twelve months—for so were the days of their anointing accomplished, to wit, six months with oil of myrrh, and six month with sweet odours, and with other ointments of the women" (Esth 2:12).

Esther, then, undergoes a typical preparatory process, leading up to her rape, a process that includes dressing up and embellishment in accordance with the proper codes in the patriarchal society.

In Hannah's case, on the other hand, not only does she not adopt these codes and does not prepare herself for the act of rape, but she does the exact opposite—she messes up her clothes and hair, that is, breaks the law and order of the culture of rape, and refuses firmly and courageously to cooperate with it.

Hanna's Undressing: Womanly Madness and Subversive Display

Undressing in public is perceived as "womanly madness"—essentially insane behavior, which Chesler[9] claims gives expression to a "body that was betrayed." She argues that women in a patriarchal society make use of their bodies to protest against oppression, especially in the context of sexual oppression. The male culture's attitude to the rebellious performance of the female body is characterized by complete indifference to the woman's furious counter-reaction. For the woman the root of this reaction is the helplessness and the severity of the injury that permeates the woman's soul and consumes it.[10] Hannah's father and her brothers

---

8. Reage, *Story of O*, 11.
9. Chesler, *Women and Madness*.
10. Gur, *Foreign Body*.

do not understand this, yet she clarifies this truth through her sharp and piercing words. She turns her naked body into a protesting and revolutionary display and ultimately it represents her rebellion against this violent, submissive and annihilating culture. According to Halpern,[11] the body may be a compass for a subversive language that provides possibilities to feminine identity and freedom that have been censored, hidden or erased in the male culture. Therefore, the body is a political site that the systems of representation of power and order try to harness as if it were a passive material subject to discipline. Yet, as Halpern writes: "The body is not only a text written by the system, it also writes it."[12] Hannah's body does not cooperate with the system. It becomes a display of fierce insubordination and deliberate disruption of the law—a wild body that can sabotage and disrupt the existing order and oppressive system.

Another issue that arises in light of Hanna's act of undressing is that her brothers call to burn her, due to the shame she has brought upon them and the Israeli public. Undressing in public is interpreted by the establishment as a kind of "obsession" (dybbuk—malicious possessing spirit)—an evil spirit that comes from the liminal marginal spheres outside the boundaries of the normative and proper sphere. These are the "middle" areas that are disgraceful and impure according to social definition. Douglas[13] argues that the definition of the abject and impure relates to a symbolic system. One, who deviates from the area of the symbolic order, "leaks" and strays beyond the margins, endangers and undermines the boundaries of the order and system. Female undressing in public may constitute a form of abjection—it threatens and violates the systemic definitions of the order. With her bare body, Hannah creates a menacing female chaos. And so, Hanna's act of undressing marks a leakage and deviation from the proper order and threatens with a chaotic, unregimented state. This state

---

11. Halpern, *Discontent Body*.
12. Halpern, *Discontent Body*, 24.
13. Mary Douglas in her book *"Purity and Danger"* analyzed the concepts of contamination, impurity, purity and taboo as social-cultural concepts.

is marked as abomination, and so the brothers are quick to denounce it outright and declare that she is to be burned, just as an abomination is burned. To set her on fire would be to consume a disgraceful, contaminated and impure matter. However, Hannah, by providing an explanation to her brothers, clarifies that what is impure is not herself, but rather the representatives of the order. She makes it clear that her brothers are the ones who are committing an act of abomination and impurity by handing her over to the ruler's bed.

Hannah, the woman who is naked in public, expresses, therefore, an act of protest and outcry. She is perceived at first as the woman who cries out, the strange and helpless woman, supposedly possessed by a bizarre spirit, yet she manages to clarify to her brothers the rationale behind her actions. This transforms the act of the supposedly "disgraceful and shameful" undressing into an act of heroism. She exposes herself naked to reveal in broad daylight the grave injustice done by her brother's when they agreed to abandon their sister, as well as the other daughters of Israel, to rape.

This is how Hannah sends out a sharp and pointed arrow of criticism not only at her brothers, but also at the listeners and readers of the midrash throughout the ages. Hannah manages to reverse the situation. Not only does she violate the decree of rape and turn from being a despised object to a purified woman, but she also transitions from being seen as a rejected woman to being a national heroine.

Summary

The chapter presents the Midrash of Hannah the Maccabee as interacting with the story of Queen Esther and as presenting an amendment to the passive obedience with which Esther accepts being handed over for the sexual use and pleasure of the ruler Ahasuerus. The Midrash, as presented, creates an inverse and revolutionary process, as it presents the absolute refusal of the feminine figure to be handed over, raped and silent about it.

Hannah breaks through the sphere of feminine silence. In light of the midrash, rape of a woman instantly becomes an issue that is being called out—it is not enabled, it is not accepted. Rape must be fought against by men and women together. Kehat notes in this context that Hannah actually redeems the text itself, so that the midrash humanizes the story of Esther. Kehat writes:

> "The encounter of a woman with feminine awareness with this text (Midrash of Hannah the Maccabee), when she is ready to express and cry out in her own voice the horror of rape from her point of view as a woman, can redeem this halacha (Jewish laws) from its androcentric boundaries, and from the severe moral distress that exists within it."[14]

But it is not only the moral distress that this Midrash redeems. It also opens the door to the process of redemption, rebirth, healing and restoration of the feminine body-soul. A significant step in healing and rehabilitating from sexual trauma is the ability to speak the crime that was committed, to give testimony and tell the pain that was inflicted and validate this consuming pain. While the book of Esther ignores and silences the sexual trauma and disgrace of the female body and soul, thus creating an offensive memory in Jewish tradition, the Midrash of Hannah provides an amendment to this violent tradition of a conventional culture of rape. The amendment is made when Hannah's story speaks the silence and fights the rape decree, and therefore gives women the healing and rehabilitative validation that sustains their wounded souls. Hannah gives women a new memory of rehabilitation—a memory that has a rebellious, subversive, non-subjugated feminine struggle, and it provides the hope of healing and transformative power in coping with the trauma and recovering from it.

14. Kehat, "The Cohen's Daughter."

Chapter 4

"If Anything but Death Parts Me from You"

The Love of Ruth and Naomi

> "Now women return from afar, from always: from 'without,' from the heath where witches are kept alive; from below, from beyond 'culture'; from their childhood which men have been trying desperately to make them forget, condemning it to 'eternal rest.' The little girls and their 'ill-mannered' bodies immured, well-preserved, intact unto themselves, in the mirror. Frigidified. But are they ever seething underneath!"[1]

VARIOUS INTERPRETATIONS WERE ASSOCIATED with the book of Ruth regarding the reasons for its creation, as well as the messages that the book was designed to convey when incorporated into the biblical canon. Licht[2] and Zinger,[3] for instance, ascribed the book

---

1. Cixous, "The Laugh of the Medusa," 137.
2. Licht, *Storytelling in the Bible*, 125.
3. Zinger, "The Objective of the Book of Ruth—Self-Defense and Self-Justification Rather than Protest and Wrangle, 12.

of Ruth with an apologetic tone, which elucidates the Moabian roots of King David and why his Moabian grandmother is more than worthy to establish the future royal lineage of the Davidic line. Kara-Ivanov Kaniel[4] argues that the book of Ruth is a central intertextual link, which focuses on the development of the messianic and the female model connected to it. Ruth refines and softens the sexual sins of her seductive female counterparts from both the moral and ethical aspects. Furthermore, Kara-Ivanov Kaniel considers Ruth's active seduction a polemic against the Christian myth of maternal abstinence and female passivity. The mother of the Messiah of the Davidic line is not a pure and holy virgin, but a real woman, who becomes a mother through sexual interaction and not by the Holy Spirit without human seed.[5]

Other researchers, such as Weinfled,[6] and Frymer-Kensky[7] argue that the book of Ruth establishes the belief in Divine Providence and fulfills the promise of the restoration and revival of Israel and the House of David. Others, like Zakovitch[8] and Fischer[9] argue that the book challenges the separatist policy, opposes the strict separation from foreigners and advocates openness toward them.

According to Avneri,[10] the book of Ruth has an educational-social objective, which is giving a voice to those found at the margins of society and those considered inferior, in both socioeconomic and gender terms. By referring to the gender aspect, Avneri continues a research point of view that considers the book as the expression of a female writer. The Book's features and characteristics—positioning women as center stage heroines, an intimate description of a female world revolving around a female axis, many dialogues taking place between women, the dominant

4. Kara-Ivanov Kaniel, *Holiness and Transgression*, 26.
5. Kara-Ivanov Kaniel, *Holiness and Transgression*, 306.
6. Weinfeld, "The Universal Trend and the Separatist Trend," 228–42.
7. Frymer-Kensky, *Reading the Women of the Bible*.
8. Zakovitch, *Ruth*, 34.
9. Fischer, "The Book of Ruth, 61–65.
10. Avnery, *Liminal Women*, 29.

"parliament" of women accompanying the story of Naomi and Ruth, a soft and gentle female atmosphere, female wisdom revealed in dialogues, the awareness of the plight of widows in terms of social status and the focus on the issues of marriage, pregnancy and childbirth—have all led researchers to conclude that it was a female author, who wrote the book of Ruth. Avnery[11] argues that the voice of the female author exposes women's ability to create a new relationship based on solidarity, grace, compassion, loyalty and love. Like Avnery, Pardes[12] also argues that the book of Ruth offers an alternative depiction to dominant biblical representation of women duos found in conflict and rivalry.

Avnery presents the duality embodied in the two possible readings of the book of Ruth—the first reveals the courage and audacity of women, who determine their own fate, manipulate men for their own purposes and detach themselves from the patriarchal context that defines their existence and their relationships. The other reading describes women who conform to the patriarchal norms and collaborate with an oppressive androcentric order.[13]

The reference to the duality of voices in the biblical story becomes even more complex in light of Dijk-Hemmes' research[14] concerning the "double voice" of the female author. Dijk-Hemmes and Brenner[15] studied the biblical texts as gender-dependent, while distinguishing between male and female texts. In light of the examination of the texts as the creation of a female author, Dijk-Hemmes identified, a double voice as typical of the female text. One voice speaks in the language of the patriarchal culture, complying with patriarchal codes, and the other speaks in the language

---

11. Avnery, *Liminal Women*, 33–34.
12. Pardes, *Countertradition in the Bible*, 79–91.
13. This optional reading matches Esther Fuchs' reading, which illustrates how the author basically forms femininity in his image, describing women that dutifully internalize the endocentric codes and presents the ratifying obedient choice as the free choice of the heroines. See Fuchs, "The Literary Characterization of Mothers and Sexual Politics, 127–39.
14. Van Dijk-Hemmes, "Final Consideration," 107.
15. Van Dijk-Hemmes and Brenner, *On Gendering Texts*.

of the "women's culture."[16] This culture relates to the social roles, activities, priorities and behavior patterns typical and unique to women's lives and their experiences as a silenced minority group. In the sphere of the hegemonic voice, the minority group's experiences have been experienced as an undefined black hole. The world of women's experience and being remains, in part, with no definition, conceptualization or formulation. Therefore, women remain silent and paralyzed. On the other hand, in spheres beyond the hegemony—in spheres of the "women's culture," named "Wilderness,"[17] women speak their experiences and voice their authentic feelings. In this sphere, their silence speaks outside the reach of the hegemonic censor.

Therefore, the voice of women is a double voice—silent in the expanses of the dominant culture but speaks itself in the sphere of the "women's culture" in the concealed layers of the text.

Examining the text of the female author as speaking a silenced female culture, in which what women say and experience is either not even recorded in the dominant cultural discourse (or considered as a "black hole" irrelevant to a meaningful definition of reality,[18]) is of a subversive nature. This women's culture undermines the hegemonic, phallocentric silencing mechanisms and prevails over the manipulations of control and power. It seeks to trace the other flickering voices, female voices, flashing in the text through cracks in the wall of denial and disregard. What emerges as a result, is a "dark continent" as defined by Cixous,[19] or a textual and experiential "wilderness" as coined by Showalter.

This chapter attempts to demonstrate that tracking those flickering and flashing voices in the book of Ruth reveals a "wilderness" or "dark continent" of erotic inter-feminine relationship, where men are "not even part of the equation."[20] In this sense, the

---

16. Van Dijk-Hemmes and Brenner, *On Gendering Texts*, 264.
17. Showalter, "Feminist Criticism in the Wilderness," 267.
18. Showalter, "Feminist Criticism in the Wilderness," 267.
19. Cixous, "The Laugh," 144.
20. As written in the context of a lesbian vaginal monologue, in Eve Ensler's book, *The Vagina Monologues*. See Ensler, *The Vagina Monologues*.

book of Ruth as a creation of the female author is a subversive work because she dares to "speak" and voice that "wilderness." She strives to show that the "dark continent" which is regarded as an intimidating sphere is in fact, as coined by Cixous, "a laughing Medusa."[21] In other words, this is a pleasurable, liberating and beneficial sphere for women.

In the next section of this chapter, I will present the following relevant concepts—"dark continent," the Irigarian dialogue of the "double lips"[22] and Rich's "lesbian existence,"[23] concerning a unique inter-feminine existence, which is usually silenced and denied in the phallocentric culture. I will then go on to explain how these concepts might shed a subversive light on the relations between Ruth and Naomi and thereby "speak the silence" of that erotic inter-feminine experience.

Inter-feminine Existence As a Rebellious Cultural Element

Cixous,[24] coined the term "dark continent" as a corporeal erotic sphere—as a realm of unique pleasures and desires—a unique feminine existential experience. Cixous argues that men have made women hate women, be their own enemies and muster their tremendous powers against themselves. She urges women to re-appropriate their unique powers and help each other express and realize it.[25] They should dare to feel the entirety of their bodily exhilaration, and erotic excitement that were dubbed by the phallocentric culture as the "vagina dentate" or the devouring medusa (the Freudian symbol of the toothed vagina petrifying the phallus). Cixous argues that returning to these authentic pleasures will

---

21. Cixous, "The Laugh," 144.
22. Irigaray, "When Our Lips Speak Together," 205–19.
23. Rich, "Compulsory Heterosexuality and Lesbian Existence," 165–90.
24. Cixous, "The laugh," 137.
25. Cixous, "The laugh," 140.

reveal that the medusa is actually laughing—it brings tremendous joy, vivaciousness and power to women's lives.

Irigaray[26] has also related to this feminine corporeal existence in her poetic essay "When Our Lips Speak Together." She points to a joint feminine mode of existence which corresponds to the feminine corporeality and the doubleness of the lips, distinctive of this corporeality. In "When Our Lips Speak Together," one female voice/body addresses another female voice/body and calls for joint disengagement and joint stripping of foreign language, foreign roles, foreign names and alienated self that women have adopted within a male-masculine order.

Irigaray goes on to argue that this false reality has coerced, imprisoned and paralyzed women. It has made them forget their authentic selves and their unique voices. In this reality, women have become devoid of themselves, manipulated objects, a consumed body destined to support men and their desires, a body which must adapt itself to the method dictated by men. The female body/voice beseeches the female addressee not to forget their joint lips-language any longer and not to miss out on each other as well as themselves. She encourages women to free themselves of all the names, rules, labels and encodings that imprison them, as women, forcing them to exist in a manner alien to their authenticity.

While men regard the lips of the woman as an organ to be used, encoded and penetrated, Irigaray describes the doubleness of the lips as an expression of a holistic mode of existence that is boundless, unlimited, unexpected, free of misconceptions and bias, expanding and spreading, having an infinite movement that encompasses openness, devotion and joint empowerment.

Irigaray's mode of existence is also depicted in Rich's formative essay "Compulsory Heterosexuality."[27] In this essay, Rich argues that men are mostly emotionally secondary in women's lives. Other women are the source of vitality and emotional support, sharing a rich emotional world of solidarity and empowerment. The inter-feminine existence is a source of knowledge and power

26. Irigaray, "When Our Lips Speak Together," 205–19.
27. Rich, "Compulsory Heterosexuality," 165–90.

available to women. It is an existence of joy, courage, sharing, complete sensuality, friendship and sisterhood. The lesbian inter-feminine eroticism is not limited to a certain organ, a certain body part or only to the body. It is all-present energy. Therefore, heterosexuality is not necessarily a woman's preferred mode of existence, because it splits between the erotic and the emotional.

Rich argues that the yearning for heterosexuality is in fact the result of social-political channeling,[28] which deprives and alienates the inter-feminine authentic energies. The lesbian existence constitutes a direct attack on the male right of access. It is perceived by the patriarchy as an act of rebellion, and so, the act of choosing a woman as a lover or partner for life, as opposed to the institutionalized heterosexuality, has, according to Rich, a feminist-political content and a liberating power.[29]

The story of Ruth and Naomi, as presented in this chapter, entails a liberating political content of that sort. Among its well-concealed folds and behind the masked roles of the mother and bride, is hidden a mental-erotic sphere, where a woman chooses another woman, as a life partner and lover.

The Book of Ruth—Making Silence Speak

The story of the book of Ruth takes place during the period of the Judges, a time of famine, chaos, violence and instability. Naomi's family immigrates to Moab due to the famine in Israel. There, Naomi's husband and two sons die—Mahlon (from the Hebrew word "disease") and Chillion (from the Hebrew word "extinction"). The choice of these names for the sons reflects their fate and is ironic nature in nature. It is as if from the outset, the role of the sons in the story was to die and fade away; leaving the stage free for the stories of the daughters (the phrase "my daughter" is repeated 10 times in the book of Ruth).

---

28. For more on this subject, see Leghorn and Parker, *Women's Worth, Sexual Economics*.
29. Rich, "Compulsory Heterosexuality," 96.

In most biblical stories, the sons, who are the successors of the patriarchal lineage, are central to the plot. The daughters are either ignored or utilized to fill a specific function in the story revolving around the sons or the fathers.[30] Therefore, naming the boys with such names implies the gender reversal unfolding in the story of the female narrator. Usually, to uncover the female version feminist researchers were forced to carry out a reversal of the plot and present the female secondary plot as the main one. Here, there is no need to employ this move, because the subversive female narrator dares to make the reversal herself. The heroines are the women and the whole atmosphere is clearly feminine; softness, tenderness, emotion, warmth, love, devotion and containment fill the story. The numerous female dialogues create the narrative fabric. Naomi directs her daughters-in-law, Orpah and Ruth, to the homes of their mothers, kisses them and wraps them in maternal warmth. In response, the "daughters" express their devotion to her.

Naomi expresses her concern for the fate and state of her daughters-in-law, addressing them with bitter self-humor and trying to convince them to abandon her:

"should I even have a husband tonight, and also bear sons" (Ruth 1:12). She smirks at her ill-fated destiny, saying that she no longer has a son/husband to grant them.

Orpah makes a logical decision and parts ways with Naomi following her statement. This only emphasizes the meaningfulness of Ruth's refusal to leave Naomi. This refusal marks her choice to move to a sphere that does not speak the patriarchal code and language. Ruth's choice to *cling* to Naomi points to the intertextual echo of the book of Genesis ("Therefore a man leaves his father and his mother and clings to his wife, and they become one flesh" [Gen 1:24]), as the equivalent of a bond of marriage.[31] Avital-Rozin[32] and Alpert[33] state that the use of the word 'cling' implies

---

30. On this subject, see the observations made by Cheryl Exum, "Second Thoughts about Secondary Characters," 79.
31. See Exum, "Plotted, Shot, and Painted."
32. Rozin, *"Wherever You Go, I Will Go"*.
33. Alpert, "Finding Our Past," 91–96.

an erotic lesbian relationship. The female narrator's decision to use this echoing word in this context may imply that there is an entry to a "twilight zone" that was usually ignored and denied. The entry marked here is an entrance to the erotic sphere of the inter-feminine existence, as was referred to by Rich and Irigaray. By rejecting the patriarchal code, Ruth opens a door for Naomi and herself to cross the threshold into the wilderness of the inter-feminine eroticism of the "women's culture" or "dark continent," as termed by Cixous.

Ruth's oath to Naomi ("Where you go I will go, and where you stay I will stay ... Where you die I will die, and there I will be buried ... if even death separates you and me," Ruth, 16–17), which is described by Alpert,[34] Duncan[35] and Avital-Rozin[36] as the equivalent of the traditional marriage oath, is a symbolic declaration of the subversive entry into those denied and silenced spheres in women's lives. Ruth expresses her absolute devotion to Naomi and declares her endless love.

The journey back to Bethlehem is a liminal period—a period "in between." Female researchers have related to such periods as periods of a unique "uterine" nature.[37] These researchers pointed to the liminal sphere as a space–time that enables and welcomes female realization and formation. Ashkenazi,[38] inspired by Lich-

---

34. Alpert, "Finding Our Past."
35. Duncan, "The Book of Ruth," 92–102.
36. Avital-Rozin, "Wherever You Go," 110.

37. The term "liminal" has different meanings for different genders. This issue was discussed by Caroline W. Bynum, who related to the liminal stage in Turner's model. Turner pointed out that in male cultural and religious rites of passage, the liminal phase is perceived as a regression phase in the lives of the boys and men. At this stage, they return to the uterine sphere—female and chaotic, powerless and detached from their inherent sense of power and control as members of the hegemony. Bynum argues that in women's culture the liminal phase is not experienced as regressive, but rather as allowing an authentic connection to female intensities and possibilities of expression that were previously blocked. See Bynum, "Women's Stories, Women's Symbols," 105–26.

38. Ashkenazy, *She Travels the Distance*, 70.

tenberg–Atinger[39] refers to this sphere as a uterine–female space and ascribes to it an experience that invites and allows release and transformation to those who have not been allowed to express their full being. It is a space "on the verge of becoming." Ashkenazi associates these experiences of 'coming into being' with the symbolism of embarking on a female nomadic journey. Embarking on such a female journey constitutes an incubation of the transformation of identity.

In the depicted period wherein men, the representatives of the patriarchy, are absent, and Naomi and Ruth walk the deserted liminal route alone, the possibility for a kind of unique intimacy, presents itself. It is a type of inter–feminine intimacy that is not permitted to express itself in times governed by social expectations and rigid prohibitions and frameworks. The nature of this intimacy in the liminal sphere corresponds to the experience of the doubleness of the lips as described by Irigaray. The unique space-time creates a present holistic relation which as previously stated, is without barriers and free of any preconceptions. This relation creates feminine erotic relationship, filled with joint openness, dedication and empowerment.

Opening to the new possibilities of this intimacy is exciting, but at the same time intimidating, and therefore—silence is formed. This is where the female narrator notes that following Ruth's announcement, Naomi ceases to speak to her. The silence echoes in the story and expresses what words cannot say: the two women know that they are walking toward a complex and problematic reality. En route, they can express their love, but once they reach their destination, they must censor their relationship and adapt it to the socially accepted norms. Ben Naftali describes this experience in her book "A Chronicle of Separation" as follows:

> "Our paths crossed, we strayed, we aligned, like birds of prey, flying and nesting. We met in our most desolate moments, in the most abandoned places. Intimately

---

39. Bracha L. Ettinger described this liminal sphere as a matrixial maternal-gestational borderspace, which dissolves self-separation and differentiated identity. See Ettinger, *The Matrixial Borderspace*.

"If Anything but Death Parts Me from You"

touching the edges of existence, places where there is no more certainty as to which is the student and which the teacher, which is the mother-in-law and which the bride, which is the older and which the younger, which is the experienced and which lacks experience, which is the mistress and which the slave, places where I am enslaved to you while enslaving you... I have met you as if for the first time, not as the mother of my husband, though I have kept you company for ten years... You were ready to accept me. In the past, all this would not have been possible. All images are evoked in my memory, one by one, all exciting and thrilling—the rocks under our bare feet, imprinted in them for all eternity, your seduction... for some things are deemed possible only on the journey to Judea, inside the tent, in the private sphere, in side roads farther away from the caravan, home, sovereignty, stability, leniency and the positive and negative commandments. However, at the end of this journey we had to adapt to the new reality and to set up a household in Bethlehem, in a disciplined environment struggling for stability, lest it should fall back into anarchy. The borders of this environment are clear-cut and well formulated... the environment in which we found ourselves was to re-challenge our decisions in relation to the external and the intimate, the possible and the impossible, with no guidance as to how to find our way between these worlds..."[40]

And indeed, once Naomi and Ruth arrive in Bethlehem, Naomi reverts their relationship back to the disciplined and regimented course, subjected to patriarchal codes. She removes them both from the wilderness of the concealed inter-feminine experience and severs them from the pleasure that Cixous describes as "the laughing Medusa." She reverts to what the hegemonic culture defines as significant, legitimate and relevant—the heterosexual relationship. Naomi concocts an economic and social survival plan by finding and "entrapping" Ruth's redeemer. From that moment on, the female double voice unfolds before the reader. One

---

40. Ben Naftali, *A Chronicle of Separation*, 18.

voice obeys the androcentric patriarchal order that normalizes the women's culture based on its needs.[41] The existential–emotional involvement of the women in this order is not authentic, but rather characterized by the "forgetting of the lips,"[42] as defined by Irigaray. In this existence women are alienated to themselves; They exist like "spoken machines ... enveloped in proper skins, but not their (our) own."[43]

The second voice is the voice of the inter–feminine existence— the lesbian existence according to Rich. This voice, which expressed itself loud and clear in Ruth's oath, in her infinite devotion and in the joint journey of the two women to Bethlehem, is now winding down, gradually reduced and diminished until it is silenced.

"And Naomi had a kinsman of her husband's, a mighty man of valour, of the family of Elimelech, and his name was Boaz" (Ruth 2:1). The narrator tells us that Naomi finds out that there is a worthy man, who is a member of her husband's family. This is how the seduction scheme that the women weave gets underway, with the objective of redeeming Ruth, as well as Naomi, from their low social standing, and economic and social detachment. Ruth consents to the plan and outlines the next step, suggesting that she would go to the field "to glean among the ears of corn" (Ruth 2:2), and Naomi of course, approves. Ruth goes to the field to attract Boaz's attention. He invites her to gather with his female workers and assures her that she has his protection. When Ruth tells Naomi about these events, Naomi instructs her how to proceed with the act of seduction. Naomi guides her to beautify and perfume herself, and to go to the place where Boaz is sleeping and to lie at his feet. Ruth carries out her mission, and when Boaz wakes up and finds her lying next to him, she professes her identity and asks him to rescue her from her condition. Boaz believes that Ruth chooses him out of obedience and devotion to the Torah of Israel and therefore calls her "woman of valor." This biblical and traditional

---

41. On this subject see Esther Fuchs' interpretation of the book of Ruth in "The Literary Characterization of Mothers and Sexual Politics," 127–41.

42. Irigaray, "When Our Lips," 208.

43. Irigaray, "When Our Lips," 205.

"If Anything but Death Parts Me from You"

phrase describes the woman, who successfully performs all her roles and duties toward her children, her husband, and her god. But the narrator reveals that in fact, Ruth chooses Boaz out of her love and devotion to Naomi: "All that thou sayest unto me I will do,"| (Ruth 3:5). In other words, on the overt level, Ruth acts out of obedience to the patriarchal order, but on the covert, Ruth acts out of her subversive relationship with Naomi.

At this stage, the two women are increasingly moving farther away from the unchartered, unappropriated "wilderness." They disconnect from their wild dark continent and enter the heteronormative hegemonic culture.

When Ruth returns home after the night of seduction, Naomi asks—"Who art thou, my daughter?" (Ruth 3:16), this question resonates the survival dualism of the female voice and may reveal the game of concealment that both women play.[44] Ruth and Naomi conceal their love and their intimacy, and so, only once Naomi is certain that they are alone, and there is no one in sight, Ruth reports of her deeds.

Naomi's question echoes intertextually to Gen 27:24, to Isaac's words to his son, Jacob: "Art thou my very son?" This question was asked in the scene where Rebecca instructs Jacob on how to deceive his father and receive the blessing. In both stories, the women weave a story of deception to prevail over the rules of the patriarchal order. In Genesis the inquiring man is the one deceived by his son, Jacob. But In the book of Ruth, the question is asked by the woman, who is not only undeceived by the woman she calls her "daughter," but also gains her collaboration. This daughter becomes "better to thee than seven sons" (Ruth 4:15), as the women of Bethlehem say at the end of the book. Their statement highlights the inter-feminine relation as a relation of emotional support and

---

44. This sentence, like the entire book of Ruth, gained many interpretations—simplistic or sophisticated. The simplistic interpretation refers to the question as a simple attempt to understand what transpired. Yet, more erudite interpretations argue that the question states an attempt to understand in what status Ruth returns, or that maybe Naomi was not certain that Ruth would return from the field due to the danger of going there alone, as reflected in Boaz' words.

loyalty, as presented by Rich and Cixous, as opposed to the male competitiveness and power struggles.[45] Usually, the male genealogy is placed in the center of most biblical stories, and is therefore perceived as the most significant and worthy, compared with female genealogy, which is rarely mentioned in the Bible.[46] Therefore, the intertextual echo and the inevitable comparison between the two types of genealogies form a rebellious message regarding the male genealogy.

According to Kara-Ivanov Kaniel,[47] the book of Ruth urges women to rediscover their physical and spiritual pertinence to the feminine genealogical chains as a response to the exile that was imposed on them in the patriarchal and patrilinear world. Evidence of this insidious message of the book can be found in the citation of the matriarchal lineage by the elders, which is quite uncommon in the Bible: "The Lord make the woman that is come into thine house like Rachel and like Leah, which two did build the house of Israel" (Ruth 4:11). In other words, the biblical story exceptionally reminds its female and male readers that those who built and founded the nation are not the son-bearing fathers, as is usually argued. The ones giving birth, constituting and establishing, are, lo and behold, actually the women—the mothers who conceived, gave birth, nurtured, established and built.

Later, the rescue plan of the two women progresses as planned and is crowned with success. Boaz and Ruth get married and have a son.

While it is clear that Ruth is the biological birth mother, Naomi is, as the narrator points out, his additional mother—"And the women her neighbours gave it a name, saying: 'There is a son born to Naomi . . .'" (Ruth 4:17). Namely, both Ruth and Naomi are perceived as the two mothers of the child, while Boaz's paternity is only mentioned in the concluding and more instrumental verses

---

45. Tough Rebecca is the weaver of the scheme, it is still the son, Jacob, one of the three patriarchs of the nation, who chooses to deceive and lie to his father.

46. See the argument made by Cheryl Exum, "The Mother's Place," 94–148.

47. Kara-Ivanov Kaniel, "Holiness and Transgression," 35.

of the Scroll, citing the patriarchal lineage from which King David was eventually born. Boaz's paternity is so marginal and technical that there is a traditional belief that Boaz died after Ruth's conception. This interpretive assumption implies that the man was not even a part of the relationship and the same-sex family that Ruth and Naomi formed.

The portrayal of the relationship with Boaz is filled with civility and kindness, but, at the same time, lacks the expressions of love, passion and burning dedication that prevailed between Ruth and Naomi. Boaz declares: "Moreover Ruth the Moabitess, the wife of Mahlon, have I purchased to be my wife, to raise up the name of the dead upon his inheritance" (Ruth 4:10). This statement makes it clear that the relations between Boaz and Ruth are strictly a legal and technical arrangement. On the other hand, the relationship between Ruth and Naomi stands out in its unique and intense emotional and intimate passion. The women of the town bear witness to this intense love by calling out: "for thy daughter-in-law, which loveth thee" (Ruth 4:15).

Summary

This chapter proposed a subversive feminist reading of the book of Ruth focusing on the double female voice that is found in the book and the erotic inter-feminine existence that can be exposed in it. Naomi and Ruth live in a society where a woman's place and position are determined in relation to the men in her life—her father, husband or brother. The social status and the ruling order dictate for women a certain type of relationship and sexuality. Yet, the book of Ruth turns the spotlight onto the world of women, which is usually pushed aside to the margins of the text. The book dares to illuminate with elusive flickering lights a world of feminine relationships and pleasure, which is not completely governed nor subdued by the world of male law and order.

In conclusion, if we examine the relevance of the book of Ruth as presented in this chapter and its subversive undertone, we will find that the voice that it "speaks" is still relevant and important even thousands of years after it was written. The phallocentric world of law and order still dominates to some extent our culture and life as women, as Irigaray writes:

> So there is, for women, no possible law for their pleasure. No more than there is any possible discourse... And if women—according to him, can say nothing, can know nothing of their own pleasure, it is because they cannot in any way order themselves within and through a language that would be on some basis their own.[48]

According to Irigaray, in the dominant phallocentric and androcentric culture and language, women cannot speak their pleasure, which remains vague and denied. The male language and its symbols command women in numerous ways to accept the denial as if it was not so.

> "Indifferent one, keep still. When you stir, you disturb their order. You upset everything. You break the circle of their habits. The circularity of their exchanges, their knowledge. Their desire. Their world. Indifferent one, you mustn't move, or be moved. Unless they call you. If they say 'come', then you may go ahead. Barely. Adapting yourself to whatever need they have, or don't have."[49]

In light of Irigaray's words, one can conclude that the female author of the book of Ruth is just as relevant today, as she breaks the circle of phallocentric and androcentric habits and refuses to be "indifferent" and to "keep still." Indeed, she does not "upset everything" nor speak openly about an explicit erotic love between her heroines, nor do her female characters, who conform to the patriarchal rules and do not revolt against the accepted order. Yet, the clues that this ancient wise woman inserts in the text, and the boldness of her female characters, allow the subversive reading, in which the female listeners/readers, back then as well as today, can feel, with a fluttering erotic touch, the exhilarating pleasure of the feminine wild continent, and the mutual vibrance of their dual lips.

48. Luce Irigaray, "When Our Lips," 95.
49. Irigaray, "When Our Lips," 207–8.

Chapter 5

Miriam the Prophetess
Bold Oppositional Leader

THE STORY OF THE salvation from Egypt is a constitutive biblical story in the Jewish religion, faith and culture. Moses is perceived as the sole chosen leader, and most of the events revolve around his initiation and leadership. The story also contains plots in which other characters operate, yet these plots are perceived as relatively secondary to the actions of the absolute leader.

One such secondary story is that of Miriam the Prophetess. The canonical text portrays her as Moses' sister, who saves his life as a baby, as accompanying his leadership in the Song of the Sea after the miracle of salvation, and as a sinful woman, who is punished by leprosy and is banished from the camp of Israel. However, there are hints in the story that Miriam is a much more central and dominant figure than it appears in the reading of the overt text.

Despite her relatively reduced representation in the story of salvation, Micah the Prophet (chapter 6 verse 4) indicates that she was sent, alongside Aharon and Moses, as the leader chosen by God, to prompt the Exodus from Egypt. In addition, the term "prophetess" attests to her being a spiritual leader, who was perceived as having a direct connection and proximity to God and as

Awake, Awake

delivering His words.[1] In other words, she is far beyond the image of the leader's sister, merely accompanying him, serving as his cheerleader. She has been perceived, at least at certain times and in certain traditions, as a pioneering, trailblazing and seminal leader.

While Moshe's leadership and vision are extensively elaborated in the biblical narrative, Miriam's leadership and vision are absent from the text. Scholars of biblical traditions assume that in the past there were probably traditions in which Miriam had a much more substantial and extensive part in the story of the salvation, but these traditions were lost, erased or censored.[2] In such cases, literary archaeological excavations are required to reconstruct traditions and meanings that were erased from the soil of the text:

The search is even more frustrating when the voices we seek to extract from the past are female voices, voices rarely recorded. This is where the investigation takes on an archaeological nature: it requires searching for fragments of potsherds and scattered remains.[3]

This chapter describes the search and collection of textual remains and "fossils" that have survived the patriarchal editing and deletion processes. By collecting and decoding of the remains I will try to re-trace the story of Miriam as a prime leader in the journey of salvation from Egypt. Through this process of deciphering, Miriam emerges as an oppositional force to Moses' reign. Since she constituted a significant political threat, she has become the aim of a "targeted killing" or public "shaming," and she is scorned and removed from the position of power, influence and leadership, as well as from her constitutive place in the tradition of Israel throughout the generations.

---

1. For discussion, see Lederman Daniely, "Revealing Miriam's Prophecy," 8–28; Kramer, "Miriam," 106.
2. Noth, *A History of Pentateuchal Traditions*, 182.
3. Pardes, *Countertraditions in the Bible*, 9.

Miriam the Prophetess

Miriam as a revolutionary freedom fighter

To fully appreciate Miriam's significance for the people leaving Egypt, we need to be attentive to the language of symbols of the ancient East, which appears clearly in the preserved story. Consider these factors—Miriam's name, her constant presence in the vicinity of water, and her midrashic symbolism as the gift of the water well given to the people in the desert journey—all point to her archetypal and cultural significance as a founding female-maternal symbol in the collective memory of the people. The fact that she is symbolized by the water motif and is identified as its equivalent, is even doubly underscored when considering that the story takes place in the arid desert on a long and exhausting journey of many years.[4]

Water is a clear symbol of life-engendering, preservation and hope. Water is related to the symbol of the containing vessel, which symbolizes the maternal womb. The contained and containing water, represents the cosmic primordial womb, especially when mentioned in the context of a high-ranking woman with a high spiritual role. The watery element in the womb represents both the protective amniotic fluid and the milk flowing from the breast. Usually, a child or a newborn baby appears next to the water. On the archetypal and symbolic levels, the child is born out of the fluidic depths of the Great Mother and is saved thanks to the protection and nourishment of the water.[5] Eliad,[6] who studied the ways in which female archetypes appear in religions and tribal rituals, pointed to the close connection between rivers and riverbanks, and the archaic character of the Great Mother and her femininity. He points out that the term "pu" in Babylonian signified both the origin of the river and the vagina, and that also in Sumerian, the word "buru" denotes both the vagina and the river.

And so, Miriam's position on the banks of the river in the founding biblical story, serves as a "lead" that can unearth the

---

4. Kramer, "Miriam," 106.
5. Neumann, *The Great Mother*; Sjoo and Mor, *The Great Cosmic Mother*.
6. Eliade, *Myth, Dreams and Mysteries*, 169.

fabric of the feminine story of the Exodus, which was not unveiled in all its significance and intensity in the male hegemonic narrative. The girl, who would grow up to be the prophetess of the people, was positioned on the banks of the river, watching over the baby Moses and providing him with a solution of nourishment and life. This attests to her being well beyond merely the "sister of Moses," that is, far beyond the character, who only supports the story of the future leader. Miriam is a mythical and vital "great womb" and a "great mother" in the life of the people. In the ancient world and the Mesopotamian sphere, the Great Womb (Recham Raba) was the name of the goddess itself, a source of life, upon whom kings and leaders were also dependent. The womb of the Great Goddess was perceived as the "home of fates," according to which the fate of life or death was determined for a tribe or a nation.[7] The mystery of the forces of the womb—physical, mythical and transformative—determined whether the tribe would multiply, survive and thrive, or wither and die. Miriam, as the symbol of water, constituted a womb—a protective, nourishing and deciding the fate of the people leaving Egypt.

The feminist research, which examined the female story of salvation within the story of the exodus, pointed to Miriam and her female collaborators—the midwives Shifra and Puah, who refuse to kill the Hebrew babies, the mother, Yocheved, who gives birth and nurses Moses, and Pharaoh's daughter and her female escorts, who adopt the baby, even though he is a Hebrew baby—as the representatives of a female-midwifery world that is responsible for the consciousness of freedom and liberation of the enslaved people for 400 years. The researchers[8] contend that the women did not act merely out of a private-maternal sentiment when fighting to save the lives of the babies, but primarily out of revolutionary public awareness. The choice to act against the oppressive and murderous decrees has revived the forces of rebellion, liberation and the desire for freedom. At a time when the male element is weakened,

---

7. Shifra and Klein, *In Those Distant Days*, 101.

8. Trible, "Bringing Miriam Out of the Shadows," 166–87; Exum, "Second Thoughts About Secondary Characters," 75–87.

Miriam the Prophetess

the boys are cast into the Nile, and the men are tortured with servitude, sinking into passivity and helplessness (Moses' father, Amram, does not even take part in his son's rescue effort), it is the women—mothers, sisters, wives and daughters—who become activists and fight for freedom and hope. In this context, Pardes[9] argues that the female choice is the insistence on a social-national vision of regeneration and birth:

> The insistence on the birth is a revolutionary act in the context of slavery. It teaches of hope for the future of the newborn, and the power to imagine a different future, without bondage and tyranny. It means transforming the birth of the oppressed into a meaningful event... The story of the birth of the ancient people of Israel is a story of trauma and recovery. The basic trauma in the national biography is bondage and the suppression of growth. But then begins a process of recovery that is bound with transforming the act of casting babies to the river, from an act that contradicts birth to an act of rescue. Yocheved, who casts her son to the Nile, does so not out of obedience to Pharaoh's decree, but as a gross violation of it.

The women, therefore, succeed in defeating the oppressive despair, creating a conscious transformation and embrace the hopes of rebirth and salvation. Furthermore, they offer a vision of life-engendering collaboration. In contrast to the masculine wars of dominance and brute force that will fill the story of the Exodus, the women, headed by Miriam, form an inter-feminine alliance that is committed to life. The feminine story sheds light on a sphere of vision and power that represents an alternative to the rule of the strength of hand and the phallic outstretched arm. The tension created between the representatives of the order and Moses' staff, and the alternative represented by Miriam, will continue to be tied in within the plot.

---

9. Pardes, *The Biography of Ancient Israel*, 26.

Awake, Awake

Miriam's dance of the sea

After rescuing the baby Moses, Miriam reappears in the Song of the Sea, following the miracle of the parting of the sea. In Exod 14:16 Moses is ordered to raise his staff and stretch his hand over the sea, to allow the crossing of the sea. These are clear phallic images, representing an array of male forces of war and violent overpowering. Opposite this array of forces, Miriam and the women take center stage for a moment, and present a parallel array, feminine in nature—" And Miriam the prophetess, the sister of Aaron, took a timbrel in her hand; and all the women went out after her with timbrels and with dances." (Exod 15:20).

Seemingly, Miriam is Moses' head cheerleader, leading all the women in a song of gratitude and praise of the miracle that he steered, guided by God. But is this deliberate impression indeed accurate? It seems that to understand the profound significance of this single verse, one should keep on "sniffing" the soil of the text and follow the ancient fingerprint that indicates that Miriam was the 'Great Mother' or 'Rechem Raba' (a great womb)—the equivalent of the Goddess in the ancient Near East.

First, it should be noted that Miriam's name (Marat-yam) attests to her perception as the 'Lady of the Sea', which corresponds to the names of the goddesses in the ancient world. The Canaanite Asherah was also called 'Athirat al Yam', namely, Asherah of the sea or the Goddess of the sea. According to the mythology, the goddess Artemis influenced the movement of the sea to stop Agamemnon, and the Egyptian goddess Isis is the patron goddess of seafarers, who held rituals in her honor aboard their ships, to receive her blessing and protection during their voyages.[10] The goddesses were named so, because they were perceived as affecting the movements of the sea, its waves and rhythms. Hence, it can be assumed that Miriam's name, which portrays her as the Lady of the Sea for the people leaving Egypt, suggests that she was perceived, at least in the earliest stages of tradition, as having superhuman

---

10. Patai, *The Hebrew Goddess*, 37; Bleeker, "Isis as Saviour Goddess."

powers, influencing the movements of the water and protecting those traversing the sea.

In addition, we should fully understand the portrayal of Miriam the prophetess dancing, drumming and singing next to the parted sea, leading the masses of women, in the context of the ancient world.

The modern interpretation, which refers to the practice of dance as marginal in the array of cultural-religious forces is a superficial and erroneous interpretation, according to Sered.[11] This feminine practice has a holistic quality and constitutes a live, mythical and unmediated encounter with the divine. Female researchers, such as Burns[12] and Lapson[13] also described dance and song as creating a communal sphere of sacred significance, which summons the divine presence to the life of female followers.

When referring to women who dance, Sautter[14] emphasizes the spiritual significance of a nonverbal, corporeal ritual expression, especially when it takes place in the female sphere, as distinct from a male sphere. She refers to Miriam's tradition as a constitutive tradition in Jewish life, a tradition that refers to the power of the female body as having a conscious-mythical value. Langer[15] also emphasizes the significance of nonverbal symbolism. She considers artistic expressions of music and rhythms that make the body sway, as mind-altering symbolic elements. Dance as a nonverbal process of ritual movement creates an experience of transcendence and is also perceived as having a transformative quality.

In the ancient world, apart from the dance itself, the drum and rhythmic drumming were attributed mind- and reality-altering meanings. In her research, which focused on female drumming in ancient Israel, Paz[16] presents many female figurines holding drums, that were found in archaeological sites in Israel. According to the

11. Sered, *Women As Ritual Experts*, 9.
12. Burns, *Has the Lord Indeed Spoken Only Through Moses?*, 39.
13. Lapson, "Jewish Dances of Eastern and Central Europe," 58–61.
14. Sautter, *The Miriam Tradition*.
15. Langer, *Philosophy in a New Key*, 15.
16. Paz, *Drums*, 76, 101.

Awake, Awake

study, drums were used as ritual objects by the priestesses and prophetesses. By drumming, the priestess could enter an ecstatic state that induces prophecies. Drumming was perceived as connecting the human with divinity and enhancing superhuman forces.

Ackerman,[17] who studied the role of the priestesses in the ancient Near East, presents in her research archaeological findings depicting Phoenician rituals held by priestesses, dancing and playing the drums. Other researchers present findings from the Yahweh cult sites, found in Deir Alla (TransJordan, thought to be the biblical Sukkot), and Tel Ira in the Negev desert. These findings include figurines of women of high spiritual stature—priestesses or prophetesses, holding drums as ritual objects.[18]

These findings illustrate that the drum was extremely dominant in female rituals. According to Ochshorn,[19] and Doubleday,[20] the figurines of the drumming women depict a fertility ritual, summoning abundance. Dasen[21] and Manniche[22] ascertain that the female drum was part of the rite of rebirth and fertility in Egypt (it should be noted that according to the biblical story, the Israelites left Egypt after a long stay of at least 400 years, and so the Egyptian religion and culture have greatly influenced their religious worship and ritual culture). Egyptian texts depict ritual drumming in honor of the mother-goddesses Isis and Hathor. Paz[23] mentions the mythological story of Gilgamesh, in which the preparation of the drum is linked to the cooperation between the god and the goddess—a cooperation that yielded a magnificent tree. The drum, then, is linked to divine power, and especially to the goddess' fertility blessing. Many Mesopotamian texts depict the high-level

---

17. Ackerman, "The Mother of Eshmunazor, Priest of Astarte," 158–78.

18. Franken, "The Excavations at Deir 'Allā in Jordan," Fasc. 4; Tadmor, "A Figurine from Tel Ira Reconsidered, Eretz-Israel," 383–87.

19. Ochshorn, "Ishtar and Her Cult," in Olsen, *The Book of the Goddess Past and Present*, 22.

20. Doubleday, "The Frame Drum in the Middle East, 101–34.

21. Dasen, *Dwarfs in Ancient Egypt and Greece*, 78.

22. Manniche, *Ancient Egyptian Musical Instruments*.

23. Paz, *Drums, Women, and Goddesses*, 95.

female drummer, taking part in the rituals dedicated to the goddess and performed in her temple.[24]

In her book "When the Drummers Were Women: A Spiritual History of Rhythm," Redmond[25] explains the connection between the drum and the sacred fertility rituals. Drumming by a woman, especially a spiritual leader dancing to its rhythm, was a sacred ritual designed to inflame and renew the blessing of fertility. Drumming, she argues, is perceived as imitating the rhythms of the womb. In her book, she describes ancient rituals that took place in Uruk, an ancient Sumerian city and one of the most important cities in Mesopotamia, where drumming ceremonies were held on moonless nights. Redmond explains that the queen/ goddess/priestess /prophetess, was responsible for administering these monthly rituals in honor of the moon and its cycles. The monthly lunar rituals were designed to follow the female menstrual cycle, which was perceived as parallel to the lunar cycles. This cyclicality was considered as filled with transformative forces. Drumming by the female spiritual leader was designed to attract the light of the missing moon, thus renewing the forces of fertility, regeneration and birth of the earth and man.

And so, the drumming, dancing, and singing performed by women, especially when conducted by a woman in a high spiritual position, were used to perform fertility rituals. This raises the question: why did Miriam the prophetess use a fertility ritual that was perceived as kindling the forces of the blood and womb, during the miracle of parting of the sea?

The answer lies in understanding the primordial perception of the unbroken connection between the female womb and the cosmic womb, along with their fluids and cycles.[26] The rhythms of the female womb and its cycles were perceived as parallel, affecting and affected by the pulsating rhythms of oceanic water movements—the seas and oceans. The drumming ritual inflamed the uterine forces and the maternal blood beat, and influenced,

---

24. Blades, *Percussion Instruments and their History*, 153.
25. Redmond, *When the Drummers Were Women*, 10; 82.
26. Neumann, *The Great Mother*.

Awake, Awake

according to the primordial belief, the cosmic movement of the water. Religious rituals conducted by the religious and community female leaders were used to predict the movement of the seas and the cycles of nature, and to muster divine intervention for their benevolent influence.

It should be noted that the miracle of the sea, which, according to tradition, enabled the Israelites to escape from Pharaoh's army, was attributed, among other things, to the phenomenon of tides, i.e. the rhythms and cycles of the sea, and their divine-wonderous synchronization.[27] If, as previously explained, Miriam's portrayal as a drumming prophetess leading masses of women is actually a description of a religious ritual designed to influence the rhythms of the seas, then it is meant to influence the movement of the tides. Miriam, the lady of the sea, conducts this ritual to prompt a divine intervention and synchronize the movement of the sea, in accordance with the needs of the people, traversing the sea.

From this we can understand that the single verse that describes Miriam the prophetess drumming, singing and leading the women of Israel, is a literary relic or textual "fossil," that when decoded according to the cultural language of the ancient world and the ancient near east, uncovers parts that were deleted from the story of the salvation. The verse is a testament to a momentous religious-female-spiritual ritual with a transformative effect and a tremendous resonance in the consciousness of the people.

The occurrence of the truly constitutive miracle in the tradition of Israel was construed as a heroic event that takes place thanks to Moses' acts of raising his hand and the rising of his phallic staff. However, the analysis presented reveals the miracle as actually having a female-uterine nature. Miriam, the spiritual leader, the "great womb" of the people, conducts and directs a female-abdominal ritual, that, along with the divine power, transforms the movements of the sea. The miracle of the sea is then revealed as a portrait of a true vaginal childbirth: the banks of the sea are changing, transforming and opening till they become the birth canal, the immense pressure and the thrusting forces through the ever-expanding, ever-opening

---

27. Buber, *Moses*, 26.

cervix, lead to the breaking of the water and a passage though the gaping banks. And finally, the people, like a baby that is born in a real, miraculous and wondrous childbirth, emerges from beyond the bloody waters, onwards to freedom . . .

In light of this, the story of the salvation from Egypt is portrayed as a midwifery-maternal mosaic, and the event by the sea is revealed as a physical and spiritual ceremony of the birth of the people, where women, take a vital, active and dominant role, just as they play central roles in the childbirth events of their own lives. The ritual dancing and singing advance the childbirth, as the one leading the process as an archetypal midwife and savior is Miriam, who saves her people with her confident hands. Pardes describes this as follows:

> Behind and against the "right hand" of the Warrior one can detect, I believe, a feminine hand: the strong magical hand of a grand Midwife drawing the newborn nation out of the depths of the sea, "the heart of the sea," into the world of the living, beyond the engulfing Flood.[28]

In light of the meanings that are revealed by this understanding of the feminine Song of the Sea and Miriam's role in leading it, the question arises as to how it is possible that her singing, as described in the text, contains only one line—an exact quote of the opening line in Moses' song. This quote creates the sense that the song of Miriam is a marginal, repetitive chorus of the song of Moses, and that the women function mainly as the background accompaniment and cheerleaders of Moses' leadership.

Researchers that have dealt with this issue, argue that there was an editorial intervention in the song, and concluded that the Song of Miriam was probably older than the Song of Moses, and it was apparently taken from her and altered to fit the male heroic model. Dijk-Hemmes writes: "we do not know if it was her song, we only know that there was a tradition in which Miriam led and sang the Song of the Sea."[29]

---

28. Pardes, *Countertraditions in the Bible*, 31.
29. Dijk-Hemmes and Brenner, *On Gendering Texts*, 40.

Miriam's song, is therefore, disrupted after only one sentence, and quite immediately, there is a quick transition to a recount of Moses' story. This truncation may reflect the attempt of the later canon editors to diminish the place of a woman as a pivotal leader in such a fundamental event in the formation of Israel's faith. This truncation also reflects Miriam's exclusion from the strongholds of authority, leadership and power, and may serve as indication to the next event in which she will appear.

"Hath the LORD indeed spoken only with Moses"

In the next event featuring Miriam, she allegedly speaks ill of Zipporah, Moses' wife, protests the exclusivity of his prophetic stature, and is punished by leprosy:

> "And Miriam and Aaron spoke against Moses because of the Cushite woman whom he had married; for he had married a Cushite woman. And they said: 'Hath the LORD indeed spoken only with Moses? Hath He not spoken also with us?' And the LORD heard it.—" (Num 12:1–2).

The reference to Zipporah as the 'cushite woman' and the undermining of Moses' stature as the sole leader are presented as unrelated, apart from the clear act of subversion against Moses. But Careful reading that does not follow, nor is deceived by the traditional, albeit too convenient, interpretation, raises another possibility.

Miriam, who had saved Moses from Pharaoh's death decree, and served as a liberating spiritual leader, leading tens of thousands of people, and even influenced the miracle of the sea, did not receive any recognition of her authority and role as a leader and savior. Zipporah, like Miriam, saved Moses' life as God wished to kill him (Exodus 4:25), thus enabling him, like Miriam, to become a leader. Moses was powerless and terror-stricken in the face of God, charging at him with the intent to kill him, and Zipporah came to his rescue. She managed to appease the wrath of God by circumcising her son. Then, the deadly attack ceased, and Moses was saved. Pardes describes Zipporah's capability to confront the wrath of God Himself, as a testament to her strength and power, and maybe even as a hint at the mythological facet of her character.[30] Despite her heroism and power (and perhaps due to them), Moses and his administration ignore her completely. Zipporah is later sent back to her father's home. Then, upon her return, her father receives Moses' warm attention, but Zipporah is completely ignored, even though she is the only reason that he is still alive and the current leader.

Zipporah and Miriam, therefore, embody an unflattering aspect of Moses' rule, to say the least. Both are heroines who save his life, yet he rewards them both with exclusion and expulsion. It should be noted that the exclusion of the two women does not necessarily relate to the personal-familial context or to the domestic sphere, but rather to the public-political sphere. Miriam and Zipporah are not weak and helpless women that depend on Moses, but are rather strong women of spiritual power, on whom Moses, the helpless one, depended in critical and formative events in his life. These women were excluded from the strongholds of power because, apparently, they posed a threat to the exclusivity of Moses' rule.

Hence, it is assumed that when Miriam mentions Zipporah, talking about the 'Cushite woman' and immediately complains of her own exclusion, she does not gossip or is resentful toward her, but rather, the exact opposite. Miriam protests against their mutual exclusion, which is in fact a forceful political act against them.

According to the prophet Micah, Miriam was a messenger Chosen by God, a prophetess and an influential leader followed by of thousands of people, therefore it is reasonable that she feels justly entitled to demand and claim recognition of her leadership and authority (one can assume that considering the killing of the male babies during centuries of slavery in Egypt, the number of daughters and women led by Miriam was greater than that of men during the Exodus). But when she makes this demand, she is severely punished with leprosy and is publicly disgraced.

30. Pardes, *Countertraditions in the Bible*.

Awake, Awake

And the question arises: is leprosy really a divine punishment, as the biblical narrator tries to contend? In her study of the tradition of the prophetesses of Israel, Gafni[31] contends that in the biblical text, leprosy appears as related to the power of prophecy. When the prophet is a leper, he is impure and cannot accept the prophecy. In other words, his spiritual power has expired. Therefore, the affliction of leprosy was used as a weapon in the wars between prophets over their territory of domination. Moses, who learned how to inflict leprosy (Exod 4:6–8) is, according to Gafni, the one who afflicts Miriam with leprosy. Her argument is based on hints in the text that point out that only after God had already left the scene, was Miriam afflicted with leprosy (Num 12:9). Gafni also mentions that Aaron turns to Moses, and not to God, with a plea to spare Miriam: " And Aaron said unto Moses: 'Oh my lord, lay not, I pray thee" (Num 12:11).

And so, is it possible that the events described in Numbers 12, as a 'force majeure', afflictions from the heavens, are a sanction imposed by the ruling order? The rise in Miriam's power among the people, causes the regime to immediately suppress her power and influence. When Miriam refuses to be merely a docile sister, with no recognition of her leadership, and challenges the exclusivity of Moses' spiritual and political authority, she is accused of committing the sins of evil gossip and arrogance and is punished with leprosy. Leprosy is a lesion in the skin that constitutes a social mark of exclusion and expulsion. For the prophetess, leprosy is a mechanism for political dispossession and subjugation, because it creates defilement, leading to ostracism and abjection. The labeling of impurity, according to Kristeva,[32] is a regulating mechanism designed to diminish the archaic maternal power—"in societies where it occurs, ritualization of defilement is accompanied by a strong concern for separating the sexes, and this means giving men rights over women," she writes. Miriam, as explained, embodies a maternal-feminine leadership, and the impurity of leprosy does bring about a very significant diminution on her power.

31. Gafney, *Daughters of Miriam*, 84.
32. Kristeva, *Powers of Horror*, 57.

Miriam the Prophetess

In addition, if we return to the images of the monster and the angel mentioned in the chapter concerning Yael's story, then, as Gilbert and Gubar argue, once the woman expresses her power and might and demands recognition of these, she loses her angel image and is labeled as a monster. When Miriam is afflicted with leprosy, she transitions from the image of the beloved and esteemed guardian angel of her brother, to a monstrous, repulsive and excluded figure.

Miriam threatens the very heart of the order, and all the hegemonic mechanisms of control and subjugation are mobilized for an act of deterrence and silencing. The message is loud and clear to all the women who follow her—any subversive and rebellious expression will be brutally crushed, while delegitimizing, shaming, and debasing it. And so, Miriam loses her public legitimacy and is stripped of her prophetic-spiritual role. Her vision and legacy are rejected and erased from the dominant theological record, and all that remains, thousands of years later, are a few descriptions of a marginal sister, reciting a song of praise to the exalted leader, that is then banished from the congregation of Israel due to her arrogance and envy.

Summary

After the reconstruction of Miriam's story, it is interesting to read again—while being very attentive and critical—Aaron's reaction to Miriam's punishment: " Let her not, I pray, be as one dead, of whom the flesh is half consumed when he cometh out of his mother's womb." (Num 12:12). Aaron turns to Moses and begs him to spare Miriam, who, according to the traditional interpretation, is compared to a stillborn. But is it Miriam? Is it really her, that is suddenly compared to a stillborn, or isn't she the one who is consistently the embodiment of the maternal-midwifery element?

Miriam, as previously described and explained, constitutes the image of a great midwife and mother who nourishes and protects the nation being born. The helpless, powerless child in the story is actually Moses, and therefore it is more likely that when

Aaron refers to a fetus, he hints at Moses, who survived only thanks to Miriam's sustenance, and constant reviving and nourishing presence. Aaron's words, therefore, may not be a plea for mercy for Miriam, but rather an act of defiance and warning to Moses. A baby, whose mother and womb are hurt, is hurt himself. Aaron warns Moses that such a demeaning and bitter strike to Miriam will bring his downfall, and he will be the one to pay a heavy price, like that stillborn. Moses apparently understands the message, because once Aaron completes his words, Moses cries out to God: " Heal her now, O God, I beseech Thee.' (Num 12:13).

Nevertheless, Aaron's prediction is fulfilled in a kind of poetic justice. Miriam, the nourishing and saturating maternal womb that was torn and severed by Moses' regime, dies in chapter 20. Immediately afterwards, as expected, it reads: " And there was no water for the congregation;" (Num 20:2). The water shortage, the lack of the well of Miriam, is immediately felt in the grievances of the people against Moses.

And in this situation, as the nation's source of vitality dries out, due to Miriam's disinheritance and expulsion, comes the downfall of Moses. The issue of water that fails him according to the overt text, and the sin against Miriam on the covert level, lead to his punishment, as he is forbidden to enter the land to which he so yearned. In her important article "Bringing Miriam Out of the Shadows," Trible summed up and clarified:

> "Miriam's death led to the downfall of Aaron and Moses ... If Miriam does not reach the Promised Land, so too will they not come. Indeed, the efforts to deny her due credit returned to Moses and Aaron like a boomerang, which is the criticism of them. As much as Miriam's slanderers have tried, they do not control the story."[33]

The slander against Miriam was engraved in the canonical story, so that the story that is learned and rooted was "his story," rather than "her story." However, a critical reading as presented in this chapter is possible and crucial in order to save Miriam from

---

33. Trible, *Bringing Miriam Out of the Shadows*, 181.

the shadow image that she was labeled with. The story that unfolds gives back to the prophetess, our nation's savior, the story that values and reveres her, and to us, the daughters of Miriam, the story that values and respects us.

Chapter 6

Pharoah's Daughter and Zipporah
The Courage to Violate the Patriarchal Decree

THE PATRIARCHAL ORDER, THE law of the father, underlies the patriarchal regime. The patriarchal system is based on a symbolic father figure, who holds the authority, sovereignty, power and control. This figure is manifested and reflected in the eternal image of God, presented as a father to his sons/people, and in the image of his emissaries—His prophets, priests or rabbis. The same applies to every father in a family, as he is perceived in the ancient and traditional world as head of the family, and the representative of the order and system. The father has exclusive mastery. He defines his laws, expectations and regulations, while the others—mothers and daughters—are expected to abide with him, obey his laws and internalize the code of their inferiority before him.

Moses is one of the founding father figures, a savior on a mission sent by the Eternal Father-God. As described in the previous chapter, Moses' regime utterly suppresses female greatness, and leadership aspirations and authority, in the form of Miriam. However, in Moses' story, besides Miriam, we can identify two other strong and powerful women, who dare to violate the Father's decree and will. By doing so, they challenge this decree and question its validity and legitimacy.

Pharoah's Daughter and Zipporah

These two characters are Pharaoh's daughter who is Moses' adoptive mother, and Zipporah, Moses' wife. The two figures are described by the biblical author in an abridged manner, very briefly and marginally, especially as opposed to the breadth and width in which Moses' character and actions are described. Moses makes no significant reference to them—no mention of any word that he says to his mother or any relationship that he has with her (the same applies to his biological mother). As for Zipporah, his wife? He sends her away, and completely ignores her when she returns with her father to the camp of Israel. Still, despite the shortness of the edited text, and despite the protagonist's utter disregard, it seems that the significance of these figures, throughout the generations, for the people has been far greater than that reflected in the overt text.

Pharaoh's Daughter—The Saving Mother

Pharaoh's daughter is described in the biblical story as Moses' adoptive mother. It is she who draws him from the Nile and raises him as her own son, thus saving his life. She cooperates with Miriam, Moses' sister, and accepts her offer to have Yocheved as his wet nurse. Consequently, jointly with the midwives, Miriam and Yocheved, she represents a life-saving force in the heritage of ancient Israel. Beyond this rescue scene, she is no longer mentioned in the story of Exodus.

However, this rare mention in Exod 2: 5–11 has left an indelible impression on the tradition of Israel, and the image of Pharaoh's daughter was engraved as a meaningful figure of kindness, salvation and protection. The midrashic name given to her is Bathiah—that is, the daughter of God in Hebrew. This name attests to the fact that the Jewish tradition has adopted the daughter of the enemy, Pharaoh, as an archetypal savior, along with Miriam the Prophetess. Researchers argue that the name that Pharaoh's daughter gives to Moses calls for the redemption of the oppressed, and therefore, the act of naming him is what gives him the power to act and to "draw" his people from Egypt. In fact, this is how

Awake, Awake

Pharaoh's daughter predicts the salvation of the people and sets off the rebirth of the Hebrew nation. Levin[1] describes various Jewish literary sources that portray Pharaoh's daughter as being etched in the memory of the sages and philosophers as a central figure in the tradition of salvation. It was argued that some of the signs of the Passover Seder (Jewish ritual feast that marks the beginning of the Passover holiday), such as the washing of the hands and the "Motzi" (blessing over the Matzah), were attributed to the daughter of Pharaoh, who went out to bathe in the river, thus saving Moses and as a result, also his people. The Midrashim of the "woman of valor" from the book of Proverbs, that were attributed to the great and wise women of the Bible, were also attributed to her image. Levin mentions the assertion of an influential thinker, Rabbi Chaim Vital, who wrote in the sixteenth century that the salvation from Egypt occurred thanks to Pharaoh's daughter. She also notes that in the Aramaic translation of 1 Chr 4:18, it is mentioned that the spirit of prophecy rested upon her. These interpretations and references, Levin argues, were written in later stages of the interpretations of the Aggada.

According to Ilan,[2] the meaning of the unique biblical phrase "night of watching" (Exod 12:42), which indicates protection of a special quality, was attributed to Pharaoh's daughter, who received special divine protection and safeguarding on the night of the plague of the firstborns. Like Levin, Ilan also notes that verses from the book of Proverbs, such as the verse 31:18: " her lamp goeth not out by night," were attributed to Pharaoh's daughter, as a sign of her exalted spiritual qualities.

The association between Pharaoh's daughter and the woman of valor in the book of Proverbs is significant, in light of the claims made by researchers[3] who argue that the entity of wisdom, as it is presented in Proverbs, is an equivalent divine feminine entity. Hence, the attribution of the verse in Prov 31:18: "her lamp goeth

---

1. Levin, *Midrashim of Batya Pharaoh's Daughter*.
2. Ilan, "Leil Shimurim" (A Night of Watching), 97–114.
3. Hadley, "From Goddess to Literary Construct," 395–99; Coogan, "Canaanite Origins and Lineage Reflections," 115–25.

Pharoah's Daughter and Zipporah

not out by night," which describes the wisdom and its eternal light, to the image of Pharoah's daughter, may point to traditions in which she was perceived as having lofty, sublime and divine qualities.

This hypothesis is also reinforced in Kadari's[4] study which reviews post-biblical literature that contains a wealth of traditions about Pharoah's daughter. In these traditions she is presented as being of principal importance, and is even called by Josephus Flavius, "Thermuthis"– a name that represents the Egyptian savior goddess, Isis. Amorai-Stark and Flusser[5] also mention the identification of Pharoah's daughter as Thermuthis, the divine mother-caregiver-wet-nurse, and as the equivalent of the Egyptian Isis. The researchers describe the process in which Pharaoh's daughter has transformed into the Egyptian Isis as a syncretic process resulting from reciprocal cultural influences and the permeation of Egyptian and Hellenistic mythological contents into the Jewish traditional stories.

The recognition of Pharaoh's daughter as the mythological Isis is further reinforced by the archaeological findings of Dura-Europos. In archaeological excavations conducted in 1928, wall paintings dated to the second century were found in the ruins of an ancient synagogue in Syria. Among these paintings was a fresco depicting the story of Moses' rescue in Egypt. The baby, Moses, who is drawn from the water, is held by a naked female figure, whose breasts and genitalia are bare, and her hands are raised in a ritual posture.

Researchers such as Goodenough[6] and Neusner[7] conclude that this painting reveals the Hellenistic and pagan influences on Judaism, although they do not necessarily agree on the degree of these influences. Goodenough refers in his article to the nude daughter of Pharaoh as the fertility goddess herself that is

---

4. Kadari, "Yael Levine, Midrashim of Bitya, the Daughter of Pharoah," 233–41.

5. Flusser and Amorai-Stark, "The Goddess Thermuthis, Moses, and Artapanus," 217–33.

6. Goodenough, *Jewish Symbols in the Graeco-Roman Period*.

7. Neusner, "Judaism at Dura—Europos," 81–102.

saving Moses. In the analysis of the painting and the nudity that it features, the female figure was compared to the Persian goddess Anahita, who is the equivalent of the Greek goddess Aphrodite, and her female escorts were deemed Greek nymphs.

However, it is possible that when trying to decipher the painting in terms of the goddess, there is no need to move away from influences that are foreign and detached from the religion of Israel. The study of the ancient religion of Israel, as well as the Bible itself, attest to the presence of a goddess at the beginning of the religion of Israel, a presence that was later defined as sin and idolatry.

Among the Canaanite, Egyptian and Mesopotamian peoples, there has always been a divine mother, who was responsible for satisfying the comforting maternal functions—she was a nourishing mother, whose breasts were filled with abundant milk for her people. She was a protective mother in her womb, as only a mother can protect, against all trouble, and promised the blessing8s of fertility and abundance to her people. Though the heralders of the Yahweh religion have labeled this ancient perception as idolatry, that brought disaster and destruction on the people of Israel, it seems that the people still followed the goddess, yearned for her, and found it difficult to relinquish her.

Manifestations of this worship can be found in the Bible, which describes the people's insistence on worshipping Asherah. In research, there are differences of opinion as to whether Asherah is a goddess at all, or a ritual object (asherim), such as a tree or sacred space, rich with vegetation.[8] Yet, many researchers believe that even if these are ritual objects, they have been dedicated to the worship of Asherah[9] In addition, the Prophet Jeremiah specifically mentions the goddess queen of heaven, as a benevolent goddess that the people worship:

---

8. Day, *Yahweh and the Gods and Goddesses of Canaan*; Day, "Asherah in the Hebrew Bible and Northwest Semitic Literature," 385–408; See also discussion in Dever, "Archeology and the Ancient Israelite Cult," 9–15.

9. Olyan, *Asherah and the Cult of Yahweh in Israel*; Gilula, "To the Lord of Shomron and Ashtarte," 129–37; Ackerman, "The Queen Mother and the Cult in Ancient Israel," 179–95.

Pharoah's Daughter and Zipporah

> As for the word that thou hast spoken unto us in the name of the LORD, we will not hearken unto thee. But we will certainly perform every word that is gone forth out of our mouth, to offer unto the queen of heaven, and to pour out drink-offerings unto her, as we have done, we and our fathers, our kings and our princes, in the cities of Judah, and in the streets of Jerusalem; for then had we plenty of food, and were well, and saw no evil. But since we let off to offer to the queen of heaven, and to pour out drink-offerings unto her, we have wanted all things, and have been consumed by the sword and by the famine. And is it we that offer to the queen of heaven, and pour out drink-offerings unto her? did we make her cakes in her image, and pour out drink-offerings unto her, without our husbands?" (Jer 44:16–19)

"The Queen of Heaven" was a popular name for the goddess in the Ancient Near East and ancient Israel. Some researchers[10] argue that it denotes the goddess Asherah, who ruled, according to the ancient perception, the elements of the sky (the army of the sky): the sun, moon and stars. According to the words of the Prophet Jeremiah himself, the goddess was greatly loved by the people, that enjoyed abundance and safety when worshipping her, contrasted with horror and terror, when abandoning her.

Dagan describes this as follows:

> Jewish literature about God throughout the ages has been shaped as literature that seems to try to conceal or obscure something—the primordial demonic character of God. But the more it hides, the more it reveals. It reveals because it is committed to its previous layers and draws from them ... The tribal story that grew out of the ancient Near Eastern traditions and became the Bible ... The story about the terrible God ... This story perhaps borne on the lips of some ancient nomads inserted like a jagged javelin in the heart of the bleeding Jewish memory ... Literature needs first and foremost the mother, the good and comforting speech of the mother on which the days of memory are based. But the Jewish ethos has

---

10. Koch, "Aschera als Himmelskönigin in Jerusalem," 97–120.

abandoned the mother in favor of the father. Is it the fragmented abyss or the abandoned Asherah? And the father? The father is a desert god who cannot be pleased or appeased, who terrorizes his sons, chases them to the ground and kills them"[11]

In biblical descriptions, it appears that the Hebrew people, express difficulty in settling for a single, stern, strict godfather, with no comforting divine mother. Like a child, who is raised and educated only by a demanding, punishing father, without the balancing comfort of a tender and caressing mother, the people also feel anguished and hungry for the figure of a spiritual mother. Yearning for, and following the goddess Asherah, as described in the Bible, conveys this hunger.

The Kuntillet Ajrud archaeological findings in northern Sinai[12] and in Hebron (Khirbet el-Qom)[13] dating back to the eighth century BCE, document the popular belief that was prevalent in ancient Israel. In the inscriptions found on these holy sites, the follower takes an oath in the names of Yahweh and his Asherah, that is, in the name of Yahweh and the goddess, his spouse. The paintings next to the inscriptions include the symbols of the goddess-mother in the Ancient Near East and in the religion of Israel: the breastfeeding cow and the symbols of the ibex standing next to a tree and its branches[14]. Hence, despite the prohibitions and warnings that the worship of the goddess is sinful idolatry, the yearning for the divine mother was intense and unbearable, affecting the spiritual-cultural-religious world of the people.

Therefore, the identification of the biblical daughter of Pharaoh as Thermosis—Isis, as shown, may be a manifestation of the way in which the yearning for a divine mother was given a solution or compensation. The goddess Isis was perceived in the culture

11. Dagan, "The Other God," 179–81.

12. Meshel et al., *To the Lord of Teman and Ashtarte*.

13. Dever, "Iron Age Epigraphic Material from the Area of Khirbet el-Kom," 139–204, 165–67.

14. Keel and Uehlinger, *Gods, Goddesses and Images of God in Ancient Israel*; Ornan, "Gods and Symbols in Israel in 600–1000 BC," 64–90.

of the region as a symbol of a benevolent and protective rescuer mother, and therefore, the human image of Pharaoh's daughter was "converted" in the souls of the believers and in their religious beliefs and rituals, into the image of an equivalent mother-goddess, who existed for them in ancient times.

If so, it turns out that Pharaoh's daughter, who appears for a moment in the biblical story, has taken a much bigger and central role in the traditions of the followers, as the Jewish religion has evolved. Her role as Moses' savior, and her sublime, high-ranking figure, were reflected in literature, commentaries, Midrashim, as well as the ritual paintings in the synagogues, so that the worshippers could feel her benevolent, protective and blessed spiritual presence.

Zipporah—A Woman of Spells?

Isis' mythological story is reflected not only in the story of Pharaoh's daughter, but also in the story of another female figure, who saved Moses, and that is Zipporah. According to the mythology, Isis' husband, Osiris, is attacked by his brother, the god Seth. He kills Osiris, chops up his body and puts it in a box. Isis, who has magical powers, is using her bird-like wings to shield her viciously attacked husband while performing a mysterious magical act on his penis, allowing his resurrection, at least to bring Horus into the world. Pardes notes this scene is like the biblical "bridegroom of blood" scene, in which Zipporah, (a bird in Hebrew), Moses' wife, saves him from God's violent and deadly attack by cutting off the foreskin of the penis (it is not entirely clear whether this is the genitalia of Moses or his son). When Zipporah cuts off the foreskin, she pronounces the words: "Surely a bridegroom of blood art thou to me ... A bridegroom of blood in regard of the circumcision" (Exodus 4, 25–26) and waves the blood of the foreskin. The vague statement that is repeated as an incantation, along with the waving of the blood, creates a sense of an enchanted magical ritual that references once again to the goddess Isis—the woman of spells.

The similarity between the stories is great, so Pardes' premise is that it is the same basic plot, and that the mythological content "permeated" into the monotheistic text. During its formation and development, the people of Israel were in constant contact with the peoples of the ancient Middle East, and its stories intermingled with the cultural values of these ancient peoples. Thus, Egyptian literature greatly influenced biblical literature.[15]

Therefore, tracking the unfoldment of stories from various ancient sources may shed light on facets that have not been sufficiently illuminated by the biblical editor. Awareness of this possible dynamics of plots and characters in the Ancient Near East raises the possibility that Zipporah's character is in fact, a certain incarnation of Isis, who rescues her high-ranking husband from the attack of a wrathful god. The two characters—beyond the great similarity in the plot—share, according to their stories, an enchanted magical power, that was able to withstand Seth's destructive power, in Isis' case, and Yahweh's sudden wrath, in Zipporah's case.

Summary

In summary, it seems both Pharaoh's daughter and Zipporah in their stories appear to be literary incarnations or equivalents of the divine goddess Isis. Hence, both the women and their stories were much more significant, extensive, and dominant in the religion of Israel and its traditions, and their importance was far more fundamental than that given by the biblical editor.

But Pharaoh's daughter and Zipporah's significant role has a challenging importance, beyond their being mythological characters. It is important to note that their act of saving is based on an action that contradicts the decree and will of the father—whether the father figure is Pharaoh, who was considered a god in Egyptian culture, or whether the father figure is the god Yahweh. Pharaoh's daughter knows that baby Moses is Hebrew, and she is supposed to let him drown in the Nile, according to her father's order. Nevertheless, she chooses to save him, and even adopt him as her son in the palace. Zipporah is found in a situation where God attacks

---

15. Talshir, *Biblical Literature*; Shupak, *No Man Is Born Wise*.

Pharoah's Daughter and Zipporah

Moses, his messenger, and tries to kill him. Generally, if God the Father believes that a certain person should be killed, then it is an act that is considered as just and necessary. However, Zipporah is unwilling to accept this, and takes a stand to save her husband. She confronts the power and wrath of God, withstands them, and tries to change the decree.

Both women save their relatives from the murderous decree of a jealous and violent king-god-father, through active and direct resistance, and violating his command. They refuse to obey the decree of death, not of Moses as a baby, nor of Moses as an adult. They stand as an equal force, disobedient, unapologetic, unhidden, fighting against the destructive, lethal force by whatever means available to them, thus expressing a demonstrative, poignant and courageous position of refusal.

That is why Pharoah's daughter and Zipporah evince a subversive stance not only against monotheistic ideology, but against the patriarchal regime, as well. Their actions and choices undermine and challenge the patriarchal order that is based on almost total control of the father figure—the divine, and the human.

Therefore, Pharoah's daughter and Zipporah present to the female reader—in the past, as in today, the possibility of refusing the patriarchal decree, and the male system. These women prove that this position of refusal is critical and vital for the fulfillment of freedom and goodness. Had they not acted boldly and daringly against the will and decree of the father, Moses would not have survived, and his vision as a savior and liberator of the enslaved people would not have been fulfilled.

Pharoah's daughter and Zipporah's legacy demonstrates that it is the recalcitrant and defiant woman, who refuses to obey and accept the orders of the system, the one who saves the fathers—the founders of justice, decrees and punishments—from the destruction they bring upon themselves, their messengers or their people.

Chapter 7

Sarah

The Fight for the Matriarchal Legacy

THE STORY OF THE Hebrew nation in the Bible bases its foundations on the male genealogy—"And Terah lived seventy years, and begot Abram . . . ." (Gen 11:26). The patriarchs/fathers are those who beget, and their histories are placed at the center. Matriarchs, so it seems, are our matriarchs primarily because they are married to the Patriarchs, God's chosen representatives and the precursors and founders of the Hebrew heritage. While the Patriarchs undergo trials of faith and initiation, the Matriarchs are portrayed as preoccupied with petty, insignificant matters, such as jealousy between the women over the husband's attention, or an attempt to please the husbands by bearing heirs.

However, the subversive studies of the researchers of the Bible and the ancient Near East, Savina Teubal[1] and Zipporah Yavin,[2] reveal a different story of the Patriarchs from the one depicted in the overt version in the book of Genesis. Teubal combines in her research knowledge relating to the laws and culture of the ancient Near East and the Mesopotamian sphere, where the stories of Genesis take place. Through the understanding of the laws

---

1. Teubal, *Sarah the Priestess: The First Matriarch of Genesis.*
2. Yavin, *Queen Sarai.*

of inheritance, the customs of the period and the ritual culture, Teubal offers a different understanding of the array of forces, the events and the motivations that drive the characters. According to this version, what the story depicts as petty jealousy between Sarah and Hagar, is in fact, Sarah's struggle for the survival of the matriarchal spiritual inheritance legacy, at a time when the patriarchy took over and overpowered this heritage.

Abraham and Sarah's story begins in Gen 11, as Abraham takes the barren Sarah to be his wife: "Sarai was barren; she had no child" (Gen 11:30). Later, God addresses Abraham directly, and crowns him as His chosen one. God promises to multiply his seed and makes a covenant of males with him. He changes his name as He also changes the name of his wife, but apart from that, Sarah is mostly the silent and passive wife. Abraham is commanded: "Get thee out of thy country, and from thy kindred, and from thy father's house, unto a land that I will shew thee" (Gen 12:1). Abraham is called upon for a formative journey of initiation, and Sarah is described as following him obediently. The narrator tells us that Abraham goes to Egypt and tells her that he will present her as his sister, so as not to endanger himself (for she is a beautiful woman, who will certainly attract the king's attention). He thus makes her sexually accessible to Pharaoh, king of Egypt—and yet, she is still silent.

After Sarah is taken to Pharaoh's palace, and probably to his bed, God punishes the king, who, in turn, compensates Abraham with great wealth and riches. This scenario is repeated also with Abimelech, king of Gerar, as Abraham introduces Sarah as his sister, and she is taken to the king's palace. When God is furious at Abimelech and punishes him, Abimelech, like Pharaoh, compensates Abraham with great wealth. However, in Abimelech's case, unlike Pharaoh's, the narrator emphasizes that the king of Gerar has not come near Sarah.

God then makes the Covenant of the Pieces with Abraham and promises him the land. Sarah, on the other hand, is described as preoccupied with family matters—her jealousy of Hagar over her pregnancy to Abraham and grumbling about Hagar's lack of respect toward her. After God's messengers bring tidings of Sarah's pregnancy and following the migration to Gerar and the incident with Abimelech, Sarah conceives and gives birth to Isaac. She then banishes Hagar and her son to the desert. The next seminal event is the binding of Isaac, when Abraham is commanded to bind his son as a sign of his love and devotion to God. Sarah is not heard at any of these events. In the next chapter, the silent Sarah dies, and Abraham eulogizes her.

Who is Sarah?

In her book "Queen Sarai," Yavin points to Sarah's elevated status in the ancient tradition of the people of Israel. She argues that the name "Sarai/Sarah" originates from the root word ש.ר.ר in Hebrew, which signifies a commanding status, a senior position and authority. Evidence of this can be identified, for example, in the biblical expression 'chiefs of the priests' ("Then arose Ezra, and made the chiefs of the priests," Ezra 10:5), or in Hebrew—'Sarei kohanim' describing people holding senior religious spiritual positions. The word 'saratu' in Sumerian, an ancient Mesopotamian language, means a queen. In Akkadian, the word 'siru' means valued and supreme. Its Sumerian equivalent 'elu' means a supreme and heavenly being.[3]

Moreover, other biblical references relating to Sarai may attest to her importance and prominence. Details that were blurred, censored and edited in the story of Genesis, have endured in other places in the Bible, from which one can learn about her prominent religious status. On the ability to draw information that was altered or blurred from various places in the Bible, Zakovitz wrote:

> "Is it really possible to read between the lines and reconstruct a tradition that was rejected or changed beyond recognition because it did not please? Because it no longer conformed to the world of the beliefs and opinions of an author or editor? It seems to me that the answer to this question is positive, and we are assisted by the method of literary archaeology... At times, we will

3. Hurowitz, "Portrait of the Mesopotamian God," 8.

find in the margins, in a textual periphery, the tradition that the Bible sought to reject from its central discourse. Sometimes the rejected dual tradition will be found even outside the historiographic field . . . to be revealed in another literary genre in the Bible, such as in the prophetic literature."[4]

Indeed, in Isaiah's prophetic literature, we can find symbolic names that reveal Sarah's religious-leadership status in the ancient tradition of Israel. The prophet calls upon the people: Look to the rock from which you were cut and to the quarry from which you were hewn; look to Abraham, your father, and to Sarah, who gave you birth ('Teholelhem' in the Hebrew text) (Isaiah 51:1–2). The prophet describes to the people its physical and spiritual foundations and infrastructure—the roots and origins of the people. He describes Abraham as the father, yet Sarah is not portrayed as one would expect from her depiction in Genesis, as a mother. Contrary to the misleading translation in English that refers to Sarah as the one giving birth, the Hebrew text, instead of calling her the mother as expected, actually refers to her as 'מחוללת'—'Meholelet'.

The interpretive tendency is to relate to the meaning of the word *teḥôlelkem* 'תחוללכם,' in this verse as a birth in the human sense, but an examination of the places where this phrase appears in the Bible reveals a more unique and special meaning.

Firstly, the verb 'מחולל' in different conjugations (תחולל, יחולל, מחולל) appears in the Bible in various places in the sense of generating and creating, in ways that are not necessarily under human control or power. For example, in Prov 25:23, it reads: "רוּחַ צָפוֹן, תְּחוֹלֵל גָּשֶׁם; וּפָנִים נִזְעָמִים, לְשׁוֹן סָתֶר." (The north wind bringeth forth rain, and a backbiting tongue an angry countenance"). In Deuteronomy 32:18, it reads:

"צוּר יְלָדְךָ, תֶּשִׁי; וַתִּשְׁכַּח, אֵל מְחֹלְלֶךָ." (Of the Rock that begot thee thou wast unmindful, and didst forget God that bore thee). Similarly, in Proverbs, it reads: "בְּטֶרֶם, הָרִים יֻלָּדוּ—וַתְּחוֹלֵל אֶרֶץ וְתֵבֵל;" (Before the mountains were brought forth, or ever Thou hadst formed the earth and the world). The use of the various inflections of the verb

---

4. Zakovitz, *Jacob*, 15–16.

'מחולל' characterizes forces of creation, conception, and formation from the foundation of a country, nation or people. The 'מחולל' or generator is a power beyond the human power. In Isaiah 66:8, there is a similar use of this verb, which appears in a slightly different way: "מִי-שָׁמַע כָּזֹאת, מִי רָאָה כָּאֵלֶּה—הֲיוּחַל אֶרֶץ בְּיוֹם אֶחָד, אִם-יִוָּלֵד גּוֹי פַּעַם אֶחָת: כִּי-חָלָה גַּם-יָלְדָה צִיּוֹן, אֶת-בָּנֶיהָ" (Who hath heard such a thing? Who hath seen such things? Is a land born in one day? Is a nation brought forth (יוחל) at once? For as soon as Zion travailed, she brought forth her children"). The word 'חלה' is the equivalent of the word "born" or "brought forth," but the birth is a mythical and non-human birth—Zion, as signifying a symbolic female entity, gives birth or creates the people of Israel. Also, in Proverbs, the 'מחוללת' appears in a similar way to that in Isaiah, as an exalted and heavenly female entity, who was close to God in ancient times, at the time when He created the world. In the book of Proverbs, we read:

> "There was still no deep when I was *brought forth* (*holalti*, חוללתי) no springs rich in water; before the mountains were sunk, before the hills I was born . . . He had not yet made earth and fields, or the world's first clumps of clay, I was there when He set the heavens into place; when He fixed the horizon upon the deep" (Prov 8:24, 26–27).

The female being in this verse describes herself as present with God, in the days when the world was not yet created—in the chaotic days when the wind blew over the void, as told in Gen 1.

And so, the usage of the verb 'מחוללת' to describe Sarah articulates a perception that Sarah was much more than a uterine vessel used to multiply the seed of the chosen father, Abraham. This usage portrays a sublime, high-ranking being, that is characterized by a very intense and intimate closeness to divinity.

It is possible to detect in the text additional indications of this exalted facet—the expression "kings of peoples shall be of her" (Gen 17:16) parallels the way in which the goddesses in Egypt and Canaan were described—Isis was the mother of kings, and Asherah is referred to as the Mother of the gods.

Sarah

Also, the links found in the Bible between the image of Sarah and the entity of Wisdom in the book of Proverbs also provide hints regarding her lofty stature. When Sarai expels Hagar and demands that Abraham do as she says, God orders Abraham to listen to whatever Sarah tells him. This might be interpreted as a divine desire for domestic peace, yet, if God does not function as a mediator in marital affairs, it is reasonable to assume that the statement in which Abraham, the patriarch of the nation, was called by God to obey Sarai, attests to the fact that her character was attributed great spiritual knowledge and wisdom. Usually, the follower is expected to heed God's words, and yet here, Abraham, the chosen Patriarch, is ordered to take heed of all that Sarah says. It seems that God himself accepts Sarai's authority. This statement echoes the words of Wisdom in the book of Proverbs: "My son, attend unto my wisdom; incline thine ear to my understanding"; (5:1). The believer is called by God to heed all that Wisdom says, just as God ordered Abram to listen to all that Sarai says. Sarai, has therefore, the prominence of the supreme divine Wisdom.

In Proverbs there is a tight correlation between the entity of Wisdom and the act of building—in Hebrew the root of the word wisdom (בינה) and building (בנייה) is the same and is written with the same letters. For example, it reads: "Wisdom hath built her house" (Prov 9:1), and in Hebrew: "חָכְמוֹת, בָּנְתָה בֵיתָהּ" and "Through wisdom is a house built" (Prov 24:3), and in Hebrew: "בְּחָכְמָה, יִבָּנֶה בָּיִת." Genesis quotes Sarai as saying: "it may be that I shall be built up through her" (Gen 16:2), and in Hebrew: "אוּלַי אִבָּנֶה מִמֶּנָּה" (built or 'אִבָּנֶה' *ebane*' in Hebrew is based on the same letters of 'בינה' *bina*' or wisdom). In other words, Sarai is described as aspiring to build her home, the same as Wisdom is described as building a home.

The equivalence between Sarah and the entity of Wisdom appears also in the writings of the commentators, who argue that Sarai is in fact, the woman of valor mentioned in Proverbs, and Philo[5] identified Wisdom in the context of Sarah, as a mother that nurses and nourishes all her followers.

---

5. Schwartzmann, "Gender Concepts of Medieval Jewish Thinkers and The Book of Proverbs," 191.

Awake, Awake

Wisdom is presented in the Bible, according to many researchers, as a divine female figure. Brenner[6] describes the female character in Proverbs as—"Lady Wisdom," and Camp[7] depicts her as a spiritual being that has undergone a process of personification. Murphy[8] refers to the depiction of Wisdom in Proverbs as a woman of valor and argues that she embodies divinity in its female form. Therefore, the equivalence between the entity of Wisdom and the image of Sarai may attest to her elevated spiritual stature.

Sarah's character embodies, then, the memory of a fundamental and well-rooted tradition in the religion of Israel of a seminal and founding mother, having spiritual authority, very close to the divinity, that may have, at some times represented a female aspect of divinity.

This conclusion reinforces Teubal's argument. Teubal[9] studied the story of the Matriarchs in Genesis. She argues that Sarah was a priestess or a 'khnt'. As such, she was committed to a tradition of spiritual motherhood. Teubal examined the stories of Genesis and concluded that the stories record the struggle of the nation's great matriarchs, chiefly Sarah, against the patriarchal attempts of taking over.

The role of the priestess is mentioned in Egyptian and Mesopotamian literature and is documented in archaeological findings from the ancient Near East.[10] The priestess was required to dedicate herself to her role, and therefore did not bear children. Bearing children and handing down the religious heritage was carried out by the woman, who was chosen by the priestess. The task of biological mothering was entrusted to other women, who served the high priestesses. This assumption, Teubal argues, explains why barreness or not having children, appears until a decisive stage and many years later, in the stories of Sarah, Rebekah, and Rachel. Sarah's words:

6. Brenner, *Israelite Women*, 41–44.
7. Camp, "Wise and Strange," 33.
8. Murphy, "Religious Dimensions of Israelite Wisdom," 453.
9. Teubal, *Sarah the Priestess*.
10. Brisch, "The Priestess and the King," 161–76; Ackerman, "The Mother of Eshmuazor, Priest of Astarte," 158–78.

Sarah

"the LORD hath restrained me from bearing;" (Gen 16:2), which were interpreted as Sarah being barren, may suggest that her role as priestess has prevented her from having children. She, therefore, gives her maid, Hagar, whom she has mentored in Egypt, to Abraham, to "be built up through her" (Gen 16:2). The term "built" that was interpreted as a desire to strengthen Sarah's status and dignity in her husband's eyes, is interpreted by Teubal as Sarah's desire to build and establish the lineage of her religious heritage.

Hagar is obligated, according to the laws of the ancient Near East, to acknowledge that her biological son is Sarah's heir, and to honor the matriarchal inheritance lineage. But the text suggests that Hagar betrays the commitment to this lineage—"her mistress was despised in her eyes" (Gen 16:4). The lineage of the maternal inheritance is tilted when Hagar treats Ishmael as Abraham's heir, and does not respect Sarah as the bequeather, whom she needs to represent. Sarah therefore identifies a danger that she will be disinherited from the position of spiritual bequeather. This process can be recognized when Abraham insists that the lineage of inheritance be focused on Ishmael—"'Oh that Ishmael might live before Thee!'" (Gen 17:18), and not on Sarah's intended son. Ishmael's circumcision (Gen 17:25), which is a male covenant that excludes and disinherits mothers from the sacred covenant with divinity, illustrates more than anything the patriarchal political and religious act of erasing the matriarchal heritage.

In light of this process, Sarah is required to become a mother herself, to have an heir. Therefore, chapter 18 contains a different version of the promise of inheritance: if in chapter 17 Abraham stands at the center of the promise and is the addressee, in chapter 18 the main addressee is Sarah. The first question that the messengers heralding the heir's birth are asking is: "Where is Sarah thy wife?" In this encounter, the focus is on Sarah in light of her future conception: "And Sarah laughed within herself, saying: 'After I am waxed old shall I have pleasure . . . ' And the LORD said unto Abraham: 'Wherefore did Sarah laugh?'" (Gen 18:12–13).

The Binding of Isaac—The Other Story

Sarah does become a mother herself and gives birth to Isaac as her successor. She devotedly continues to preserve Isaac's stature against elements that threaten this exclusivity, by dismissing Hagar from her position and banishing Ishmael. Isaac represents the spirit of Sarah's heritage. A clear indication of this is the action Isaac takes when Rebekah first arrives and he takes her to Sarah's tent: "And Isaac brought her into his mother Sarah's tent, and took Rebekah, and she became his wife; and he loved her. And Isaac was comforted for his mother" (Gen 24:67). Teubal believes that the tent, where Sarah is also found when the birth messengers arrive ("and Sarah heard in the tent door" 18:10), is of a cultic ritual and religious significance. This tent is the equivalent of the reed structure with the triangular angular roof, which served in the ancient Near Eastern religions, as the worship and dwelling place of the goddess Inanna/Ishtar. This structure served as the home of the priestesses and religious leaders and was called "sarrat-e-ki-ur." Isaac, the successor of Sarah, the "meholelet," brings his bride to his mother's place of worship. Rebekah, then, alongside Isaac, is intended to continue the spiritual-religious heritage of the mothers.

The binding decree, though presented in the patriarchal text as posing a threat to the legacy of Abraham's seed, actually relates also to the inheritor of Sarah's legacy. The text reports the binding incident as the story of Abraham, the bearer and founder of the new faith: "And He said: 'Take now thy son, thine only son, whom thou lovest, even Isaac, and get thee into the land of Moriah; and offer him there for a burnt-offering upon one of the mountains which I will tell thee of'" (Gen 22:2), but does not report about the binding as the story of Sarai, the bearer and founder of the new faith. According to the story, it seems that the trials of faith do not concern the matriarch of the nation, or maybe they are beyond her capabilities and spiritual and mental readiness.

The Canonical text, then, leaves Sarah out of this seminal, constitutive story. She is not summoned, nor does she respond, and her silence cuts like a knife and clutches the heart and womb of the woman-mother-reader.

Sarah

So, was Sarah indeed silent? What about the ancient traditions transmitted orally or in drawings and images? Has the "meholelet," the mother in a prominent stature, the bearer of the new Hebrew faith, completely vanished or become dumbstruck in the story of the binding of her son? Was she really silent and absent in these horrifying decisive moments?

Unraveling Sarah's divine and sublime facets, as presented above, may unearth faded traces and censored passages that have been omitted from the story of the binding, and thus may provide answers to these resonant questions.

According to the overt text, when Abraham raises the knife to slay Isaac, Sarah's heir, a divine voice calls him, stops the killing and directs him to a ram caught in the thicket. Abraham is ordered to take the ram and bind it instead of the son. The ram caught in the thicket is described by the narrator as a mere random occurrence in itself, but in fact, this is a powerful symbol in the ancient Hebrew religion. The ram and the thicket were the widespread symbol of a divine female being. Keel and Uehlinger,[11] prominent researchers of the iconography of the ancient Near East and the ancient Hebrew religion, report that the symbols of the horned animals like ibex or ram standing next to tree branches or shrubs, are central motifs identified in many ritual sites, where the mother-goddess was worshipped. These symbols signified the fertility, harmony, protection and abundance provided by the goddess. Ornan[12] has also recognized the symbol of the ram and tangled branches, like the thicket described in Genesis, as a symbol of the worship of an exalted female being that bestows blessings and protection.

The language of the symbolism of the ancient Near East tells, then, the tale that was not included in the biblical canon. The timeless icon of the ram and the tree attests to a component in the ancient story that was apparently erased from the edited tradition—a spiritual mother figure, who was later represented by the iconography of the ram and the thicket, has saved Isaac's life, in one way or

---

11. Keel and Uehlinger, *Gods, Goddesses and Images of God*; Keel, *Goddesses and Trees.*

12. Ornan, "Gods and Symbols in Israel in 600–1000 BC," 64–90.

another. She may have even done so at the price of her own life, for the ram was bound to the altar and slain instead of Isaac.

The biblical narrator does not mention this event, but in the chapter following the story of the binding, he reports that Sarah has died.

This story of the courageous motherly rescue is absent from the tradition of Israel, but it seems that its memory echoes throughout the generations and ages of the Jewish people, as each year, on the second day of Rosh Hashana (the Jewish new year), the shofar (musical instrument of ancient origin, made of a horn, traditionally of a ram) is blown and the story of the Binding of Isaac is read out loud in the synagogues. According to biblical commentators, the sound of the shofar conveys Sarah's heart-wrenching sobs, grief and misery as she learns about her son's binding attempt.

The shofar, the horn of the ram, the remnant of the symbol of the ram and the tree signifying the protection of the spiritual mother, reminds and resonates, every year, the untold story. Perhaps the story was censored, because in it, the Patriarch Abraham is revealed as failing both morally and humanly, and the paradigm of patriarchal heroism and sacrifice is revealed as distorted, frightening, and terrifying.

Isaac was saved, but his mother was killed, and that marked the beginning of the end of matriarchy. Fathers and sons were placed at the center of the political, cultural, religious, ritual and national worlds, while mothers and daughters were disinherited, excluded, and marginalized.

And still, it seems that despite the impeachment attempts, it was impossible to wipe out the main evidence that the first Matriarch, Sarah, and not the Patriarch, Abraham, was perceived as the herald and bearer of Israel's faith and religion. The midrash of the name of the people of "Israel," according to the author of the book of Genesis says that Jacob rose to the challenge and fought God: 'for thou hast striven with God and with men and hast prevailed' (Gen 32:29). "Striven" in the Hebrew text appears as Sarita 'שרית'—and that is why Jacob, and subsequently, the people, were named Israel.

Sarah

Yet, scholars[13] have rejected the feasibility of this explanation as the authentic source of the name, arguing that it is unlikely that God will be the predicate and not the subject in the name, and it is unlikely that the name will document the defeat of God. And so, if the origin of the name "Israel" that is presented by the biblical author, is not a reasonable and authentic explanation, then what is this explanation concealing, and what is it trying to hide?

The Midrash presented by the biblical author to the name of the Jewish people is probably intended to obscure the fact that the source of the name is the name of the founding matriarch of the people. Her name was etched and engraved, together with the name "El," in the name of the people for all eternity. The combination of "El" and "Sarai" (El+ SARAI) became in reverse order, typical of theophoric names, to "ISRAEL" (in a similar process where for example, the name "El-yakim" became "Yehoyakim" and "Yakemyahu").[14] As a result, it turns out that it is Sarai, not Abraham, who is portrayed in the patriarchal canonical story as the protagonist, who was engraved in the name of her people as the proclaimer of the Hebrew faith.

It seems that despite the efforts to reduce and diminish her image, the name "Israel" will continue to attest to the fact that the Sarai, the Matriarch, the "meholelet," the central, main and predominant founder of the faith of Israel and the people of Israel, was well and far beyond what the biblical narrator was willing or prepared to admit.

---

13. Kogut, "Midrashic Derivations Reading the Transformation of the Names Jacob and Israel," 219–35.

14. Tur-Sinai, *El Shadday, Eretz-Israel*, 40.

Chapter 8

The Lover in Song of Songs
Sexual Boldness and Subversive Feminine Pleasure

Almost everything is yet to be written by women about femininity: about their sexuality, that is, its infinite and mobile complexity, about their eroticization, sudden turn-ons of a certain miniscule-immense area of their bodies; not about destiny, but about the adventure of such and such a drive, about trips, crossings, trudges, abrupt and gradual awakenings, discoveries of a zone at one time timorous and soon to be forthright. A woman's body, with its thousand and one thresholds of ardor-once, by smashing yokes and censors, she lets it articulate the profusion of meanings[1]

> I, too, overflow; my desires have invented new desires,
> my body knows unheard-of songs . . . I, too, have felt
> so full of luminous torrents that I could burst[2]

---

1. Cixous, "The Laugh of the Medusa," 134–54, 144.
2. Cixous, "The Laugh of the Medusa," 136.

The Lover in Song of Songs

FOR GENERATIONS, FEMALE SEXUAL needs, desires, fantasies, rhythms and ranges of sensation, have been censored as taboos of shame and guilt. And when feminine sexuality was allowed to be present and be heard, it was on the condition that it focused on the phallus and its desires, or as Katherine MacKinnon puts it: "To be clear: what is sexual is what gives a man an erection. Whatever it takes to make a penis shudder and stiffen with the experience of its potency is what sexuality means culturally."[3] The criterion to what is defined as "sexy" is what arouses the man, and what will make his penis get to work.

Women's sexual liberation in this age is reflected in the re-appropriation of their sexuality and their bodies. Women are finally articulating their authentic sexual experiences—abusive and oppressive experiences, alongside experiences of discovery, passion, desire and pleasure. This array of experiences reflects a process of seeking authentic identity and shaping female selfhood within a culture, religion, and society, in which female sexuality has been defined, regulated, and tamed according to male restrictions, laws and needs. The focus of the present feminist era is on the feminine experience—what sexually stimulates women, what arouses them, what is good for them and what improves their personal wellbeing. Women dare to examine what they really need in order to express themselves and the yearnings of their bodies.

Alongside descriptions of bleeding sexual assaults, that are being exposed and revealed, and despite alienated, paralyzing and weakening experiences, women insist on celebrating their passions and the fire burning between their legs. Since women are born with a unique organ in their bodies—the clitoris, which is designed for no other purpose than pleasure, and since this organ contains a huge number of nerve connections that allow for tremendous sexual pleasure, in a wide array of forms and sensations, it can be determined that the female body is born to be sexual, pleasured and inflamed with passion.

The roots of sexual repression are found in the theological perception based on the Scriptures. Eve seduces Adam using her

3. MacKinnon, "Sexuality, Pornography and Method," 137.

feminine charms and makes him eat from the tree of knowledge. This tree actually signifies sexuality, since the use of the word "to know" is often used in the Bible to describe sexual intercourse. Sexual intercourse is embodied in the fruit of the garden, which is an ancient symbol of lust and sexual desire, and indeed Eve attests that the tree—"was a delight to the eyes" (Gen 3:6) and in Hebrew תַאֲוָה-הוּא לעיניים, where תַאֲוָה literally means passion or desire. Eating the fruit, namely, seduction and active feminine sexuality, leads to the expulsion of Adam and Eve from the Garden of Eden, and to the punishment and suffering of all humanity. Therefore, feminine seduction and desires are, according to the book of Genesis, the source of the original sin and human suffering. And so was engraved, as early as the story that lays down the laws of nature, a negative attitude laden with guilt and shame toward feminine sexual drives, which ostensibly justifies the need and the necessity to exercise mechanisms of control, taming and supervision over the woman's sexual life.

This suppressing message is particularly prominent in the Prophets' literature, in which the image of a sexually active woman in pursuit of her desires was presented as signifying the people of Israel in its lowest states of spiritual and disgraceful decline. The Prophets of the nation—Ezekiel, Isaiah, Hosea, and Jeremiah present such a woman as a prostitute, whore, adulterer and sinner. Jeremiah calls: "upon every high hill and under every leafy tree thou didst recline, playing the harlot" (Jer 2:20). The prophet Ezekiel says: "But thou didst trust in thy beauty and play the harlot because of thy renown, and didst pour out thy harlotries on every one that passed by; his it was" (Ezek 16:15), and "and hast opened thy feet to everyone that passed by, and multiplied thy harlotries" (Ezek 16:25). And he goes on to say: "Wherefore, O harlot, hear the word of the LORD! Thus saith the Lord GOD: Because thy filthiness was poured out, and thy nakedness uncovered through thy harlotries with thy lovers; and because of all the idols of thy abominations..." (Ezek 16:36). In this verse, the prophet clearly describes the vaginal fluid of feminine desire (Nehushteh

The Lover in Song of Songs

in Hebrew, and in English: "filthiness") as a sign of the woman's abominations and great shame.

The descriptions are metaphorical and designed to illustrate the betrayal of Israel, the woman, her husband, God, but the metaphor of Israel as a harlot or a whore that is repeated time and again as a dominant and striking motif, establishes and reinforces the humiliating, offensive, diminishing and demeaning representation of female sexual desire. The woman's bodily expressions and fluids become symbols of sin and shame. These meanings are intensified by the description of the speaker in the book of Lamentations, who presents the gushing and erupting female sexuality as ultimately bringing heavy punishment, abuse, destruction and annihilation, not only for the woman herself, but also for her children. This is how the 'humiliation scale' is delineated and engraved. According to this scale, women are being punished, and pay a tragic and heavy price for sovereign expressions of sexuality. Wild, passionate, active feminine sexuality, then, justifies, according to biblical descriptions, revulsion and petrifying punishment, and is destructive and calamitous equally on a personal, spiritual, and national level.

It should be noted that there are a few cases in the Bible in which female sexual initiative is presented in a relatively positive light, as in the stories of Tamar or Ruth. The women in these cases seduce men to have sex, but it is not their authentic desire that guides them, but the need to survive within the patriarchal family order. As a weakened class with no authority or sovereignty, their sexuality is an essential survival strategy, sometimes the only one, with which they can save themselves and stabilize their status. The biblical author, followed by the readers, is tolerant of this sexual activism, because it confirms and reiterates the rules of the patriarchal order, and justifies its goals—bearing male heirs, and in Ruth's case, the establishment of the Davidic monarchy, several generations later.

Feminine desire and pleasure in themselves, then, are not described in the Bible as meaningful or essential, but they are also presented as negative, leading to sin and moral corruption. However, between the pages of the Bible, along with the slanderous descriptions, there is a celebration of feminine desire. It turns out that in our sacred, holy book, there is a woman with a bursting and raging sexuality, totally awake and burning with desire. This character is singing her songs of passion together with her lover, in the Song of Songs.

Celebration of Feminine Pleasure, and Sexual Sovereignty

The text of the Song of Songs has been largely interpreted in a conservative manner, reading it as expressing a deep and emotional love, but one that "conforms to the conservative rules" and is supervised by those who uphold and enforce the patriarchal order (the keepers of the walls, Song 5:7). In this type of love, there is no consummation or sexual intercourse in practice. Despite vivid descriptions of the female lover's abundant breasts and the curves of her thighs, she remains pure and a virgin: "A garden shut up" (Song 4:12). Even when her lover knocks on her door, and she stands naked on the other side of the door (Song 5:3), and opens it filled with passion, still, the sexual encounter does not take place, according to the explicit description. The yearning, at least on the overt level, is presented as a "pure" profound desire, which enabled the various commentators to explain that the Song of Songs presents a poetic metaphor for the relationship of yearning and love between the people and God.

However, under the conservative veil, which monitors the text and its interpretation in accordance with the needs of the hegemonic power and control, a subversive and rebellious meaning prevails. To uncover it, one needs to decipher the code of the symbols embedded in the text. It is important to bear in mind that the literature, culture and art of the ancient Near East have greatly influenced the biblical literature and the culture of ancient Israel. Mesopotamian and Canaanite content, symbols, narratives and practices permeated the culture of Israel and the Holy Scriptures and inseparably intertwined. Therefore, knowledge of ancient Near Eastern culture and literature is essential for a more accurate and correct understanding of biblical stories, writings and poetry. This knowledge will enable us to identify various other senses and denotations that the traditional commentators were not necessarily willing to admit.

The study of ancient Near Eastern culture, and especially the study of the poetry of ritual love and erotic art, provide a key to decoding the ancient language of erotic symbols.[4] This key allows for the lifting of the pristine veil from the platonic relationship. Then, what is awakened and revealed in its full glory is a rousing and passionate erotic show, with wild and daring female eroticism in its core. In this performance, the woman is active, the initiator, the one pining, touching, delighted and overflowing, and she is not embarrassed to tell her female audience about it.

One of the most striking and surprising features of the emerging erotic performance is the sexual sovereignty displayed by the woman speaker, over her body and desires. This sovereignty is bold and daring even in terms of the liberated woman in the twenty-first century. The bold protagonist of the Song of Songs, dares, as I will illustrate, to ask her lover to hurry and penetrate her with his erect penis, and to pleasure her. The body for her is a site of pleasure and intoxication. She allows herself to be uninhibited and celebrate her juicy, curvaceous body in full light with open, liberated and natural boldness.

Before reading the Song of Songs, one must become familiar with an important symbolic principle that must be noted when trying to decode the code of symbols in the text. This principle is the parallel, which is found in ancient Near Eastern literature and culture between the human body and an architectural structure. The structure of the house or the temple was perceived as the equivalent of the human body. The openings of the house symbolize the openings of the body, and the doors, the doorstep, and the gates are parallel to the female genitalia. Therefore, the door served as a common metaphor for fertility, pregnancy and childbirth. This can be recognized in biblical expressions relating

---

4. Pope, *Song of Songs*; Patai, *Man and Temple*; Assant, "Sex, Magic and the Liminal Body," 27–51.

Awake, Awake

to the functions of fertility and the womb in the context of opening or closing of the door, for example: "but the LORD had shut up her womb" (1 Sam 1:5).

The garden, the hill, and the vineyard are additional symbols of the female organs associated with fertility. Flowers and vegetation are prominent symbols of the goddess's power of passion, and they were drawn and engraved alongside the triangle of her genitalia, symbolizing sacred female power. The vegetation, flowering and the ripening, on the hills, the mountains, the gardens, and the vineyard—were all linked to the erupting female force of sexuality and bountiful fertility. Hence, the numerous descriptions that appear in the Song of Songs depicting entering or staying in a garden or vineyard, entering and exiting through gates, knocking on doors or moving between chambers—all these and more insinuate in a poetic language to physical and sexual acts.

Other erotic symbols are the intoxicating drink that appears in erotic reliefs, which the woman sips toward intercourse or during penetration, and honey, which represents the sweet fluids of the vagina stimulated before the orgasm. The vaginal fluids secreted during the arousal and pleasuring of the woman were called honey and butter, since they were pleasure-inducing. This is how the love honey is described in Sumerian love poetry—

> Bridegroom, let me caress you,
> My precious caress is more savoury than honey,
> In the bedchamber, honey-filled,
> Let me enjoy your goodly beauty,
> Lion, let me caress you.
>
> My precious caress is more savoury than honey.
> Bridegroom, you have taken your pleasure of me,[5]

When we, as readers, are more aware of the map of ancient erotic symbols, we can read the Song of Songs while lifting the restraining veil of "respectability and righteousness." Then, we can encounter the female sexuality—our sexuality—as it erupts

---

5. Shifra and Klein, *In Those Distant Days*, 340–41.

The Lover in Song of Songs

unrestrained, takes the floor and sounds her voice, and her roar of pleasure.

In chapter 1, the female lover asks her lover to kiss her, and claims that his love is better than wine. As previously explained, the wine as an intoxicating beverage appears in the ancient art next to a couple found in a state of sexual arousal, sometimes in coitus, when the woman drinks the intoxicating fluid during the lovemaking. The mention of the drink creates the erotic context of the lovers' dialogue, within the sphere of arousal and sexual amusement. The male lover, Shulamite says, takes her to his chambers and they drink from the wine. She asks for his whereabouts and looks for him, and he calls her to come to him. The seeking games are used as a flirtatious foreplay, as her lover scans her body very closely, praising, admiring and flattering her beauty. She describes her perfumed breasts and hints at the scent of the "cluster of henna" or "Camphire" (Song 1:14), found in her vineyard. The Camphire, or henna tree, is the plant from which the ritual red henna is produced, which is used to this day for weddings and other celebrations. This plant is an ancient symbol of desire, joy and fertility, and the female lover mentions it as found in her "vineyard," which, as previously mentioned, like the "garden," symbolizes the female intimate organs—the vagina and the uterus. The vagina corresponds to the flowers and fruit that are like aphrodisiacs in the garden, and the womb corresponds to the fertile and fruitful soil in the vineyard. By describing the "vineyard" of her body that awakens for her lover, the Shulamite directs her lover to their bed ("also our couch is leafy," Song 1:16). She describes the beams and cedars, which signify strength and phallic rigidity, along with her vineyard—her genitalia—that are aroused at his words and touch.

Chapter 2 opens with the presentation of the female lover as a lily or a rose, whose petals are spread and gaping. The flower, as aforementioned, symbolizes the female genitalia and the labia of the vagina, which spread and gape open. The female lover, therefore, is awaiting open and ready for her lover. She describes him as an apple tree that she covets. As she tastes from his fruit, and from him, they sip wine, and she says that "his banner over me is love" (Song 2:4). Again, as aforementioned, the couple drinking the intoxicating drink is found in a sexual and erotic sphere, toward, or at the time of penetration, and so the expression "his banner over me is love." (In Hebrew the word for "banner" is a flag), implies that the lover's penis is erect and upright like a flag, facing the woman, who yearns to taste it and feel it. The ecstatic moment draws near, when she declares: "Stay ye me with dainties, refresh me with apples; for I am love-sick" (Song 2:5).

After the climax, she describes her lover embracing her, while they calm down and relax together. She then addresses her audience of women, the "daughters of Jerusalem," to whom she recounts her sexual experiences, and asks them not to rush her love and lover, and wait for his desire to rise again—"I adjure you, O daughters of Jerusalem, by the gazelles, and by the hinds of the field, that ye awaken not, nor stir up love, until it please." (Song 2:7).

Then, in chapter 2, verse 8, after the request to wait for the awakening of love "until it please," it seems that the lover's desire, as well as his penis, are awakening—"Hark! my beloved! behold, he cometh, leaping upon the mountains, skipping upon the hills," (Song 2:8). The game of love begins again—"behold, he standeth behind our wall, he looketh in through the windows, he peereth through the lattice (Song 2:9) . . ." The male lover praises again his beloved and describes the entire nature awakening as they become aroused: "The flowers appear on the earth; the time of singing is come . . . The fig-tree putteth forth her green figs, and the vines in blossom give forth their fragrance" (Song 2:12–13). The description of nature—"O my dove, that art in the clefts of the rock, in the covert of the cliff, let me see thy countenance, let me hear thy voice;" (Song 2:14) which is supposedly a search for the hidden lover, also embodies the search and exploration of her body and her pleasure organs hiding in "in the covert of the cliff," to hear the sounds of her sexual pleasure.

At this stage the vineyards and their intoxicating scent are mentioned, illustrating the joy of intoxicating love, and the sexual harmony is described as "My beloved is mine, and I am his, that feedeth among the lilies" (Song 2:16).

The Lover in Song of Songs

The next sex scene is described in chapter 3, when the woman describes herself in her bed at night filled with longing and desire for her lover. She seeks him in the streets and brings him to her home and to her bed. Thus, in chapter 4 as well, the act of love continues when the man glorifies the beautiful body of his beloved, praising her breasts, and saying: "Until the day breathe, and the shadows flee away, I will get me to the mountain of myrrh, and to the hill of frankincense"(Song 4:6).

From stroking the beautiful breasts of his female lover, he moves on to delighting her "hill of frankincense," dripping with honey and milk: "Thy lips, O my bride, drop honey—honey and milk are under thy tongue;" (Song 4:11). Honey, as previously explained, is used to describe the sweet arousal fluids flowing from between her legs, the more aroused and stimulated she becomes. This surging arousal is also conveyed in her depiction as "a fountain of gardens, a well of living waters, and flowing streams from Lebanon" (Song 4:15). In the moments of ecstasy that take place in her garden "Awake, O north wind; and come, thou south; blow upon my garden," (Song 4:16), his penis also exudes its liquid in her garden: "that the spices thereof may flow out. Let my beloved come into his garden" (Song 4:16).

Another sexual encounter is described in chapter 5, when the male lover tries to awaken his beloved. He comes to her garden, intoxicated by her honey and wine, and probably tries to rouse her for a sexual act. She describes herself as lying in her bed, as if asleep, but her heart, she says, is awake. The man tries to get her to open her door, that is, to allow him to penetrate her "my beloved knocketh: 'Open to me, my sister, my love' . . ." (Song 5:2). She plays "hard to get," says that she has gone to sleep and toys with him: "I have put off my coat; how shall I put it on? I have washed my feet; how shall I defile them?" (Song 5:3). The male lover, on the other hand, "put in his hand by the hole of the door, and my heart was moved for him" (Song 5:4). The hole is supposedly the keyhole or the door hole, but it clearly hints at her genitalia, which is craving for him. In the Hebrew version it reads: "וּמֵעַי, הָמוּ עָלָיו." The English version uses the word "heart," but in Hebrew, it implies the womb, as in the book of Ruth, Naomi says: "have I yet sons in my womb" (Ruth 1:11), which in the Hebrew version reads: "הַעוֹד-לִי בָנִים בְּמֵעַי." All of the Shulamite's female organs, she reveals, are burning with passion and yearning in anticipation for the hand of her lover to penetrate and please her. When she opens her door-body for him, she says: "and my hands dripped with myrrh, and my fingers with flowing myrrh, upon the handles of the bar" (Song 5:5). Her hands are dripping with arousal fluids from touching the outer area of her genitalia (the lock on the door)—the touch of the man's fingers, as well as her own.

Reading the Song of Songs, while being aware of the ancient erotic symbolism and its implications relating to the bold and audacious sexual descriptions in the text, raises the question of how this text was included in the biblical canon. As I mentioned earlier, many scholars and commentators have debated this issue, and the prevalent explanation is that the yearning and longing is a metaphor for the people's longing for God. Yet, the erotic scenes are so vivid, intimate, physical and daring, and the descriptions of penetration, self-pleasure, and mutual pleasure are so tangible and graphic, that it is hard to believe that they were not intended to portray an actual erotic act of lovemaking. Therefore, I would like to suggest a different explanation.

In the ancient cultural perception, sexual arousal, and more specifically female sexual arousal, was perceived as having a transcendental and divine effect. Drawings and reliefs of a marked and accentuated vagina triangle were found in religious ritual sites, as well as in Yahweh's places of worship, and were identified as representing abundance, fertility and blessing. In sacred sex rituals held in the Mesopotamian world, the king was expected to sexually please the goddess, or the priestess representing her, to bring blessing to his country. As the king passed between the gates—the sacred labia of the goddess Inanna (Ashtar or Queen of Heaven), after he had pleased and satisfied her, he was spiritually elevated and achieved the ability and the right to govern and be benevolent to his country. This physical pleasure was perceived as creating a harmonious and abundant existence not only for the divine lovers, but also for the people and the land.

The sexual pleasure accompanied by the vaginal wetness, and the honey and myrrh fluids that emanate from between the legs of the woman, were perceived as bringing blessings and benevolence to the soil, turning it into a moist, fertile and "satisfied" land. The germination of the seeds, the blooming of the flowers, and the ripening of the fruit and crops—all these were associated with the sexual arousal and pleasure. The orgasmic experience signified a heightened and heavenly state of consciousness, and an optimal and powerful existential state of abundance, prosperity and life energy at its peak.

As explained above, despite the attempt to present the culture of ancient Israel as disassociated from the Canaanite and Mesopotamian cultural environment, in effect, there was no such separation. The culture of Israel and its religion have absorbed much of the cultural and literary content of the Canaanite environment, until various elements were adopted completely, that they were merged and assimilated into the Hebrew religion and culture. A striking example of this is found in the most formative salvation story of the Jewish religion. The exodus from Egypt and the journey through the desert for 40 years represents one of the harshest, most difficult, as well as most constitutive periods of the people of Israel, which is found in the midst of consolidating its faith. To inspire the people, boost their hope and their spiritual and mental resources, they are promised "a land flowing with milk and honey." This expression is used to describe the Promised Land, to which the people of Israel yearn to enter after the excruciating journey in the desert. If we examine the timeless expression that describes the land, we will discover how inherent the ancient perception relating to the connection between female sexual arousal and abundance and prosperity is. The use of the verb "flow," as Pardes also argues, is characteristic of the description of physical phenomena and of bodily secretions. If the milk might suggest the land as a breastfeeding mother, then the honey suggests, as explained, physical-feminine pleasure. In other words, God and Moses, according to the text, use expressions of female sexual arousal that were common in ancient times, to signify the bountifulness and abundance that will prevail in the land to which the people are journeying.

The promise, then, of a land flowing with milk and honey, is the promise of a land full of Eros, whose body is like the body of an aroused woman, who exudes her honey of love with infinite abundance.

The fact that the symbol of female sexual arousal was chosen to encourage the people and bolster them in harsh moments of hopelessness, despair and crisis, attests to the profound, essential and crucial nature of this symbol in the consciousness of the people, as a symbol of hope and benevolence. Hence, relinquishing the Song of Songs, as a text that focuses on arousal and sexual pleasure, might have largely been a relinquishment of an ecstatic text that led believers to a consciousness of abundance, prosperity and optimal life. When the people read the Song of Song's text, they could feel the joy of life, the vitality and the pleasure that oozed from it like a flowing spring. When they sang it repeatedly, they could experience the celebration of the senses that filled it. The Song of Songs is a poetic impassioned text that imparts its readers with an experience and sense of wellbeing, blessing and goodness, which is apparently why it was included in the biblical canon.

The concept of feminine pleasure as positive and blessed, and of feminine arousal as related to a benevolent, powerful and prosperous state, was obscured, concealed and eradicated in the patriarchal religions. The lustful and sovereign feminine pleasure turned into a "black hole," not too substantial and quite marginal in the spiritual and cultural life. The phallic erection and male penetration, as signifying power and conquest, were placed at the center of the religious and cultural stage.

Nevertheless, as I have demonstrated in Sarah's story, the symbols that have constituted a spiritual anchor in the mind of the people, and fulfilled a profound and essential need, or served as the foundation of its faith, have persisted, despite the eradication efforts, and left a testament and a trace. Despite the efforts to silence it, the women's roar of sexual pleasure, is heard to this day

The Lover in Song of Songs

on Sabbath eve, when the verses of the Song of Songs, along with their bold female sexuality, are read and sung in synagogues. The female lover of Song of Songs continues, therefore, to lavish and bestow her blessings of benevolence and abundance, arousing the congregation of male and female worshippers, to fulfill the commandment of "Oneg Shabbat"- Joy of Shabbat.

Chapter 9

Epilogue

It becomes clear that our ancestral mothers have gone beyond and even surpassed, the place and role assigned to them by the men, who edited, adjusted, and later regulated their stories. Our ancestral mothers were not, nor did they aspire to be obedient, docile, "angelic" women of valor. In truth they knew how to preserve the wild and tempestuous boldness of the "monster" or the "witch," as presented in the chapters of this book. It was not the timid demureness, the passivity, the quietness or the introversion, that were the ideals that guided them and their spiritual path, but rather the boldness, the subversion and the insistence on protest, rejection and defiance—saying "no," even if, under the circumstances, it was sometimes a limited, partial or covert response.

The presence of this subversive stance in the stories of our ancestral mothers is like a knock on an inner door that evokes a deep, ancient and vital memory. Our protracted captivity in millennia of a patriarchal world seems to have erased the paths of memory to this fearless maternal heritage. A lengthy neglect and disregard have caused this memory to sink almost into oblivion. However, once we meet the stories again and experience the intensity of the fury and protest of our mothers, as well as their passionate desire and fiery boldness, we realize how much we have forgotten. How

Epilogue

much we were made to forget, and yet, how, despite everything, we had not been defeated.

Yael and Deborah, Hannah, Ruth, Miriam, Tzipora, Sarah and the heroine of Song of Songs—earthly and divine women, creators, midwives, warriors, priestesses and prophetesses—a partial, but miraculous feminine mosaic is the primordial ground on which our religion and culture were formed. This land was conquered by the patriarchy and its agents, it was robbed and stripped of its resources and properties, but nevertheless, when we dare to wake up—to challenge and undermine the exclusivity of the patriarchal ancestral heritage, we find again, in the depths of its womb, the gifts and treasures of the maternal heritage.

Bibliography

Ackerman, Susan. "The Mother of Eshmuazor, Priest of Astarte: A Study of Her Cultic Role." *Die Welt des Orients*, Bd. 43, H. 2 (2013) 158–78.
———. "The Queen Mother and the Cult in Ancient Israel." In *In the Hebrew Bible*, edited by A. Bach, 179–95. New York: Routledge, 1999.
Adler, Freda. *Sisters in Crime: The Rise of the New Female Criminal*. New York: McGraw-Hill, 1975.
Adler, Rachel. *Engendered Judaism*. Tel Aviv: Yediot Ahronot, 2008.
Alpert, Rebecca. "Finding Our Past: A Lesbian Reading of the Book of Ruth." In *Reading Ruth: Contemporary Women Reclaim a Sacred Story*, edited by Judith A. Kates and Gail Twersky Reimer, 91–96. New York: Ballantine Books, 1994.
Ashkenazy, Shaula. *She Travels the Distance: Journey and Passage as Generating Female Writing*. Tel Aviv: Wrestling, 2012.
Ashman, Ahuva. "Women in the Bible as Victims of War," *Beit Mikra: Journal for the Study of the Bible and Its World* 2 (2003) 169–83.
Assant, Julia A. "Sex, Magic and the Liminal Body in the Erotic Art and Texts of the Old Babylonian Period," *Sex and Gender in the Ancient Near East, Actes de la XLVIIe Rencontre Assyriologique Internationale (Helsinki, 2–6 July 2001)*, edited by Simo Parpola and Robert M. Whiting, 27–51. Helsinki, 2002.
Avnery, Orit. *Liminal Women: Belonging and Otherness in the Books of Ruth and Esther*. Jerusalem: Shalom Hartman Institute, 2015.
Bach, Alice. "Signs of the Flesh: Observations on Characterization in the Bible." In *Women in the Hebrew Bible*, edited by Alice Bach, 351–65. New York: Routledge, 1999.
———. *Women, Seduction and Betrayal in Biblical Narrative*. Cambridge: Cambridge University Press, 1997.
Bal, Mika. *Death and Dissymmetry: The Politics of Coherence in the Book of Judges*. Chicago: University of Chicago Press, 1988.
———. *Narratology: Introduction to the Theory of Narrative*. Toronto: University of Toronto Press, 1985.

Bibliography

Ben Naftali, Michal. *A Chronicle of Separation: On Deconstruction's Disillusioned Love*. Tel Aviv: Resling, 2000.

Bird, Phyllis. "The Place of Women in the Israelite Culture." In *Ancient Israelite Religion: Essays in Honor of Frank Moore Cross*, edited by Patrick D. Miller et al., 397–419. Philadelphia: Fortress, 1987.

Blades, J. *Percussion Instruments and Their History*. New York: F.A. Preger, 1970.

Bleeker, C. J. "Isis as Saviour Goddess." In *The Saviour God: Comparative Studies in the Concept of Salvation*, edited by S. G. F. Brandon, 25–40. Manchester: Manchester University Press, 1963.

Bordo, Susan. *Unbearable Weight: Feminism, Western Culture and the Body*. Berkeley: University of California Press, 1995.

Brenner, Athalya. *Exodus to Deuteronomy, A Feminist Companion to the Bible*. Sheffield: Sheffield Academic Press, 2000.

———. *Israelite Women: Social Role and Literary Type in Biblical Narrative*. Sheffield: JSOTS Press, 1985.

Brisch, Nicole. "The Priestess and the King: The Divine Kingship of Šū-Sî of Ur," *Journal of the American Oriental Society* 126 (2006) 161–76.

Buber, Martin. *Moses*. London: West Library, 1946.

Burns, Rita. *Has the Lord Indeed Spoken Only Through Moses? A Study of the Biblical Portrait of Miriam*. Atlanta: Society of Biblical Literature, 1987.

Bynum, Caroline W. "Women's Stories, Women's Symbols: A Critique of Victor Turner's Theory of Liminality." In *Anthropology and the Study of Religion*, edited by Robert L. Moore and Frank E. Reynolds 105–26. Chicago: Centre for the Scientific Study of Religion, 1984.

Camp, C.V. "Wise and Strange: An Interpretation of the Female Imagery in Proverbs in Light of Trickster Mythology," *Semeia* 42 (1988) 33.

Chatman, Seymour. *Story and Discourse*. Ithaca: Cornell University Press, 1978.

Chesler, Phyllis. *Women and Madness*. Tel Aviv: Zmora Bitan Publishing, 1987.

Cixous, Helen. "The Laugh of the Medusa," *Learning Feminism: Fundamental Articles and Documents in Feminist Thought*, edited by Dalith Baum et al., 134–54. Bnei Brack: HaKibbutz Hameuchad Press, 2006.

Coogan, Michael David. "Canaanite Origins and Lineage Reflections on the Religion of Ancient Israel." In *Ancient Israelite Religion: Essays in Honor of Frank Moore Cross*, edited by Patrick D. Miller Jr. et al., 115–25. Philadelphia: Fortress, 1987.

Dagan, Haggai. *The Other God: Studies in Several Demonic Performances of God in Biblical Literature*. Rishon Lezion: Am Oved, 2016.

Dasen, V. *Dwarfs in Ancient Egypt and Greece*. Oxford: Clarendon, 1993.

Day, John. "Asherah in the Hebrew Bible and Northwest Semitic Literature." *Journal of Biblical Literature* 105 (1986) 385–408.

———. *Yahweh and the Gods and Goddesses of Canaan*. Sheffield: Sheffield Academic Press, 2002.

Day, M. Linda. *Esther*. Nashville: Abingdon, 2005.

Bibliography

Dever, W.G. "Archeology and the Ancient Israelite Cult: How the Khel-Qom and Kuntillet Ajrud Ashera's Texts have Changed the Picture," *Eretz-Israel: Archaeological, Historical and Geographical Studies* 26 (1999) 9–15.

———. "Iron Age Epigraphic Material from the Area of Khirbet el-Kom," *HUCA* 40–41 (1969–70) 139–204, 165–67.

Dijk-Hemmes, V., and Athalya Brenner. *On Gendering Texts: Female and Male Voices in the Hebrew Bible.* New York: E.J. Brill, 1996.

Douglas, Mary. *Purity and Danger: Analysis of the Concepts Contamination and Taboo.* Tel Aviv: Resling, 2010.

Doubleday, Veronika. "The Frame Drum in the Middle East: Women, Musical Instruments and Power," *Ethnomusicology* 43 (1999) 101–34.

Duncan, Celena M. "The Book of Ruth: On Boundaries, Love, and Truth." In *Take Back the Word: A Queer Reading of the Bible*, edited by Robert E. Goss and Mona West, 92–102. Cleveland: Pilgrim, 2000.

Dworkin, Andrea. *Intercourse.* Tel Aviv: Babel, 2003.

Eliade, Mircea. *Myth, Dreams and Mysteries: The Encounter between Contemporary Faiths and Archaic Realities.* New York: Harper and Row, 1960.

Elior, Rachel. *Grandmother Didn't Know to Read and Write: On Learning and Illiteracy, On Slavery and Liberty.* Jerusalem: Carmel Books, 2018.

Ensler, Eve. *The Vagina Monologues.* New York: Villard, 2001.

Ettinger, Bracha L. *The Matrixial Borderspace.* Minneapolis: University of Minnesota Press, 2006.

Exum, Cheryl. "The Mother's Place." In *Fragmented Women: Feminist Subversions of Biblical Narratives*, edited by Cheryl Exum, 94–148. Sheffield: JSOT, 1993.

———. Plotted, Shot, and Painted: Cultural Representations of Biblical Women. Sheffield: Sheffield Academic Press, 1996.

———. "Second Thoughts about Secondary Characters: Women in Exodus." In *Feminist Companion to Exodus to Deuteronomy*, edited by Athalya Brenner, 62–75. Sheffield: Sheffield Academic Press, 1994.

Fischer, Irmtraud. "The Book of Ruth: A Feminist Commentary to the Torah?" In *Ruth and Esther: A Feminist Companion to the Bible*, edited by Athalya Brenner, 61–65. Sheffield: Sheffield Academic Press, 1999.

Flusser, D., and S. Amorai-Stark. "The Goddess Thermuthis, Moses, and Artapanus," *Jewish Studies Quarterly* 1 (1993) 217–33.

Franken, H. "The Excavations at Deir 'Allā in Jordan," *Vetus Testamentum* 10, Fasc. 4 (1960).

Frymer-Kensky, Tikva. *Reading the Women of the Bible: A New Interpretation of their Stories.* New York: Schocken, 2002.

Fuchs, Esther. "The Literary Characterization of Mothers and Sexual Politics in the Hebrew Bible," In *Women in the Hebrew Bible*, edited by Alice Bach, 127–41. New York: Routledge, 1999.

———. *Sexual Politics in the Biblical Narrative—Reading the Hebrew Bible as Woman.* Sheffield: Sheffield Academic Press, 2013, 17.

Bibliography

———. "Who Is Hiding the True? Deceptive Women and Biblical Androcentrism." In *Feminist Perspectives on Biblical Scholarship*, edited by Adela Yarbro Collins, 137–44. Chico: Scholars, 1985.

Gafney, Wilda C. *Daughters of Miriam: Women Prophets in Ancient Israel*. Minneapolis: Fortress, 2008.

Gilbert, Sandra M., and Gubar Susan. *The Mad Woman in the Attic: The Woman Writer and the Nineteenth-Century Literary Imagination*. New Haven: Yale University Press, 1979.

Gilula, Mordechai. "To the Lord of Shomron and Ashtarte," *Yearbook of the Study of Ancient East, Vol. 3* (1979) 129–37.

Goodenough, E.R. *Jewish Symbols in the Graeco-Roman Period, Volume 9*. New York: Pantheon, 1964.

Gottlieb, Freema. "Three Mothers," *Judaism* 30 (1981) 194.

Gur, Anat. *Foreign Body*. Tel Aviv: Hakibbutz Hameuchad, 2015.

Hadley, Judith. "From Goddess to Literary Construct: The Transformation of Asherah into Hokmah." In *Feminist Companion to Reading the Bible: Approaches, Methods And Strategies*, edited by Athalya Brenner-Idan and Carole Fontaine, 395–99. Sheffield: Sheffield Academic Press, 1997.

Halpern, Roni. *Discontent Body*. Tel Aviv: Hakibbutz Hameuchad, 2013.

Herman, Judith. *Trauma and Recovery: The Aftermath of Violence—from Domestic Abuse to Political Terror*. New York: Basic,1992.

Hochman, Baruch. *Character in Literature*. Ithaca: Cornell University Press, 1985.

Hurowitz, Avigdor Victor. "Portrait of the Mesopotamian God." In *Gods of Ancient Times: Polytheism in Israel and its Neighbors*, edited by M. Kister et al., 1–34. Jerusalem, Ben-Zvi Institute Press, 2008.

Ilan, N. "Leil Shimurim" (A Night of Watching)," *Beit Mikra: A Journal for The Study of The Bible and Its World* 46 (Booklet B) 97–114.

Irigaray, Luce. *This Sex Which Is Not One*. New York: Cornell University Press, 1985.

———. "When Our Lips Speak Together." In *This Sex Which Is Not One*, 205–19. New York: Cornell University Press, 1985.

Kadari, T. "Yael Levine, Midrashim of Bitya, the Daughter of Pharaoh; Rebecca Tiktiner's Simhat Torah Poem," *Nashim: A Journal of Jewish Women's Studies & Gender Issues*, 14 (2007) 233–41.

Kara-Ivanov Kaniel, Ruth. Trans. Eugene D. Matanky. *Holiness and Transgression: Mothers of the Messiah in the Jewish Myth*. Tel-Aviv: Hakibbutz Hameuchad, 2014.

Keel, Othamar. *Goddesses and Trees, New Moon and Yahweh*. Sheffield: Sheffield Press, 1998.

Keel, Othamar and Christoph Uehlinger. *Gods, Goddesses and Images of God in Ancient Israel*. Minneapolis: Fortress, 1998.

Kehat, Hannah. "The Cohen's Daughter, the Decree of the Rape and the Hasmonean Rebellion." In *Voice Your Voice: Studies in the Cycle of the Year and the Weekly Torah Portions* 103–7. Jerusalem: Reuven, 2009.

Bibliography

Keren, Nitza. *Like a Sheet in the Hand of the Embroideress: Women Writers and the Hegemonic Text—An Interpretive Reading in Women's Literary Texts Based on Post-Modernism, Post-Structuralism and Post-Colonial Feminist Theories*. Ramat-Gan: Bar-Ilan University, 2010.

Koch, Klaus. "Aschera als Himmelskönigin in Jerusalem," *UF* 20 (1988) 97–120.

Kogut, Simcha. "Midrashic Derivations Reading the Transformation of the Names Jacob and Israel According to the Traditional Jewish Exegesis: Semantic and Synthetic Aspects." In *Tehillah le-Moshe: Biblical and Judaic Studies in Honor of Moshe Greenberg*, edited by Mordechai Cogan et al., 219–35. Winona Lake: Eisenbrauns, 1997.

Kramer, Phyllis Silverman. "Miriam," in Athalya Brenner, *Exodus to Deuteronomy*, 106; Sheffield: Sheffield Academic Press, 1997.

Kristeva, Julia. *Powers of Horror: Essays on Abjection*. Tel Aviv: Resling, 2005.

Langer, Susanne. *Philosophy in a New Key: A Study in the Symbolism of Reason, Rite, and Art*. (6th ed.). Cambridge: New American Library, 1954.

Lapson, Dvora. "Jewish Dances of Eastern and Central Europe," *Journal of the International Folk Music Council* 15 (1963) 58–61.

Lederman-Daniely, Dvora. "From Your Blood You Will See God: The Vital Components of Jewish Feminist Theology," *Gender: A Multidisciplinary Academic Journal of Gender and Feminism* 3 (2014).

———. "I Arose a Mother in Israel: Motherhood as a Liberating Power in the Biblical Stories of Miriam and Deborah. In *Motherhood in Antiquity*, edited by Dana Cooper and Claire Phealan, 19–20. Cham: Palgrave Macmillan, 2017.

———. "Revealing Miriam's Prophecy," *Feminist Theology* 25 (2016) 8–28.

Leghorn, Lisa and Katherine Parker, *Women's Worth, Sexual Economics and the World of Women*. Boston: Routledge and Kegan Paul, 1981.

Levin, Yael. *Midrashim of Batya Pharaoh's Daughter. An Accompanying Study for the Seder Night*. Jerusalem: Levin, 2003.

Licht, Jacob. *Storytelling in the Bible*. Jerusalem: Magnes, 1986.

MacKinnon, Katherine. "Sexuality, Pornography and Method: Pleasure under Patriarchy." In *Learning Feminism: Fundamental Articles and Documents in Feminist Thought*, edited by Dalith Baum et al., 137–50. Bnei-Brack: HaKibbutz Hameuchad, 2006.

Manniche, L. *Ancient Egyptian Musical Instruments*. Munich: Deutscher Kunstverlag, 1975.

Meshel, Zeev, et al., *To the Lord of Teman and Ashtarte: Inscriptions and Drawing from Kuntillet Ajrud (Teman Ruins) in Sinai*. Jerusalem: Ben Zvi, 2015.

Meyers, Carol. "Women and the Domestic Economy of Early Israel." In *Women in the Hebrew Bible*, edited by Alice Bach, 36–48. New York and London: Routledge, 1999.

Murphy, R.E. "Religious Dimensions of Israelite Wisdom." In *Ancient Israelite Religion*, edited by Patrick Miller et al., 450–65. Philadelphia: Fortress, 1987.

Bibliography

Neumann, Erich. *The Great Mother: An Analysis of the Archtype.* Princeton: Princeton University Press, 1991.

Neusner, J. "Judaism at Dura—Europos." *History of Religions* 4 (1964) 81–102.

Noth, Martin. *A History of Pentateuchal Traditions.* Englewood Cliffs: Prentice Hall, 1972.

Ochshorn Judith, "Ishtar and Her Cult." In *The Book of the Goddess Past and Present,* edited by C. Olsen, 16–28. New York: Crossroad, 1990.

Olyan, Saul M. *Asherah and the Cult of Yahweh in Israel,* Society of Biblical Literature Monograph Series 34. Atlanta: Scholars, 1988.

Ornan, Tallay. "Gods and Symbols in Israel in 600–1000 BC." In *Gods of Ancient Times: Polytheism in Israel and its Neighbors,* edited by Menahem Kister et al., 64–90. Jerusalem: Yad Izhak Ben-Zvi, 2008.

Pardes, Ilana. *The Biography of Ancient Israel: National Narratives in the Bible.* Tel Aviv: Hakibutz Hameuhad, 2001.

———. *Countertraditions in the Bible: A Feminist Approach.* Tel Aviv: Hakibbutz Hameuchad, 1996.

Patai, Raphael. *Man and Temple: In Ancient Jewish Myth and Ritual.* New York: Ktav, 1967.

———. *The Hebrew Goddess.* Detroit: Wayne University Press, 1978.

Paz, Sarit. *Drums, Women, and Goddesses: Drumming and Gender in Iron Age II.* Fribourg: Academic Press; Göttingen: Vandenhoeck & Ruprecht. 2007.

Pinkola Estes, Clarissa. *Women Run with Wolves.* Tel Aviv: Modan, 1997.

Pope, Marvin. *Song of Songs, The Anchor Bible.* Garden City: Doubleday, 1977.

Prince, Gerald. "Introduction to the Study of the Narratee." In *Reader–Response Criticism,* edited by Jane Tompkins, 7–25. Baltimore: Johns Hopkins University Press, 1980.

Reage, Pauline. *Story of O.* Bnei Brak: Hkibutz Hameuhad, 2003.

Redmond, Layne. *When the Drummers Were Women: A Spiritual History of Women.* Brattleboro: Echo Point, 2018.

Rich, Adrienne. "Compulsory Heterosexuality and Lesbian Existence." In *Blood, Bread, and Poetry,* 165–90. New York: Norton, 1994.

———. *Of Woman Born.* Tel Aviv: Am Oved, 1989.

———. "When We Dead Awaken: Writing as Revision." *On Lies, Secrets and Silence: Selected Prose 1966–1978.* New York: Norton, 1979.

Ross, Tamar and Jerome Gellman. "The Implications of Feminism on Orthodox Jewish Theology," in *Multiculturalism in a Democratic and Jewish State,* edited by Mauthner Menashe et al., 441–43. Tel-Aviv: Tel-Aviv University Press, 1998.

Rozin, Avital. *"Wherever You Go, I Will Go": A New Reading of the Relationship between Ruth and Naomi.* Yehud: Ofir Bikurm Press, 2012.

Sautter, Cia. *The Miriam Tradition: Teaching Embodied Torah.* Chicago: University of Illinois Press, 2010.

Schwartzmann, Julia. "Gender Concepts of Medieval Jewish Thinkers and the Book of Proverbs," *Jewish Studies Quarterly* 7 (2000) 191.

Bibliography

Sered, Susan. *Women As Ritual Experts: The Religious Lives of Elderly Jewish Women in Jerusalem.* New York: Oxford University Press, 1992.

Shemesh, Yael. "'Yet he Committed No Act of Sin with Me, to Defile and Shame Me' (Judith 13:16). The Narrative of Judith as a Corrective to the Narrative of Yael and Sisera." *Shnaton: An Annual for Biblical and Ancient Near Eastern Studies* 16 (2006) 159–77.

Shin, Shifra, and Klein, Jacob. *In Those Distant Days: Anthology of Mesopotamian Literature in Hebrew.* Tel Aviv: Am Oved, 1996.

Showalter, Elaine. "Feminist Criticism in the Wilderness." In *The New Feminist Criticism: Essays on Women, Literature and Theory,* edited by Elaine Showalter, 243–70. London: Virago, 1986.

Shupak, Nili. *No Man Is Born Wise: Ancient Egyptian Wisdom Literature and its Contact with Biblical Literature.* Jerusalem: Bialik Institute, 2016.

Sivan, Hagit. *Between Woman, Man and God: A New Interpretation of the Ten Commandments.* Bloomsbury: T & T Clark International, 2004.

Shifra Sh. and J. Klein. *In Those Distant Days: Anthology of Mesopotamian Literature in Hebrew.* Tel Aviv: Am Oved, 1996.

Sjoo, Monica and Barbara Mor. *The Great Cosmic Mother: Rediscovering the Religion of the Earth.* San Francisco: Harper & Row, 1987.

Spivak, Gayatri Chakravorty with Elaine Rooney. "In a Word, Interview," *Differences* 2 (1989) 124–56, 145.

Stocker, Margarita. *Judith—Sexual Warrior: Women and Power in Western Culture.* New Haven: Yale University Press, 1998.

Tal, Ilan. "Dance and Gender in the Ancient Jewish Sources," *Near Eastern Archaeology* 66 (2003) 135–36.

Tadmor, Miriam. "A Figurine from Tel Ira Reconsidered, Eretz-Israel: Archaeological," *Historical and Geographical Studies* 9 (2009) 383–87.

Talshir, Tziopra. *Biblical Literature: Introductions and Studies.* Jerusalem: Yad Ben-Zvi, 2011.

Teubal, Savina. *Sarah the Priestess: The First Matriarch of Genesis.* Athens: Ohio University Press, 1984.

Trible, Phyllis. "Bringing Miriam Out of the Shadows," *A Feminist Companion to Exodus to Deuteronomy,* edited by Athalya Brenner, 166–87. Sheffield: Sheffield Academic Press, 1993.

———. "Depatriarchalizing in Biblical Interpretation." In *The Jewish Woman: New Perspectives,* edited by Elizabeth Koltun, 217–40. New York: Schocken, 1976.

Tur-Sinai, Naftali. *El Shadday, Eretz-Israel: Archaeological, Historical and Geographical Studies, 3.* Jerusalem: Israel Exploration Society (1951, 1954) 40.

Van Dijk-Hemmes, Fokkelien and A. Brenner. *On Gendering Texts: Female and Male Voices in the Hebrew Bible.* New York: E. J. Brill, 1996.

Weinfeld, Moshe. "The Universal Trend and the Separatist Trend During the Return to Zion (Shivat Tzion)". *Tarbiz Journal* 35 (1974) 228–42.

Wolf, Naomi. *Vagina.* London: Virago, 2012.

Bibliography

Woolf, Virginia. *A Room of One's Own*. Tel Aviv: Yediot Aharonot, 2004.
Yavin, Tzipora. *Queen Sarai*. Tel Aviv: Resling, 2014.
Zakovitch, Yair. *Jacob: Unexpected Patriarch*. New Haven: Yale University Press, 2012.
———. *Ruth: Introduction and Commentary, Miqra' le-Yisra'el*. Tel Aviv: Am Oved and Magnes, 1990.
———. "Sissera's Tod." *ZAW* 93 (1981) 364–74.
Zinger, Osnat. "The Objective of the Book of Ruth—Self-Defense and Self-Justification Rather than Protest and Wrangle: Re-examination Following the Teachings of Jacob Licht in the Study of the Biblical Story." In *Fifty Years for the Study of the Dead Sea Scrolls*, edited by Gershon Brin and Bilha Nitzan, 23–36. Jerusalem: Yad Izhak ben Tzvi, 2001.

www.ingramcontent.com/pod-product-compliance
Lightning Source LLC
Chambersburg PA
CBHW050835160426
43192CB00010B/2037